To Karin, love

P.B.

Xmas 1964

The Lichtenberg Reader

Franz Mautner, Professor of German at Swarthmore College, is one of the world's two or three internationally recognized authorities on Lichtenberg. He has studied Lichtenberg's writings and life for twenty-five years and is one of the few men ever permitted to examine the personal papers in the Lichtenberg Archive at Göttingen University. Dr. Mautner studied at the universities of Vienna and Heidelberg, and received his Ph.D. from the University of Vienna. He has recently decoded and published, in German, selections from the Lichtenberg diaries. He is the author of two books on German literature and theater and has contributed numerous articles to American and German journals.

Henry Hatfield, Professor of German and Chairman of the Department of Germanic Languages and Literatures at Harvard University, has been interested in German literature of the eighteenth and twentieth centuries both as a student and teacher. A graduate of Harvard, he studied at the universities of Oxford and Berlin and holds an M.A. and a Ph.D. from Columbia University, where he taught for several years. He is the author of WINCKELMANN AND HIS GERMAN CRITICS; THOMAS MANN; and SCHNITZLER, KAFKA, MANN (with J. M. Stein).

The Lichtenberg Reader

Selected Writings of
Georg Christoph Lichtenberg

Translated, Edited, and Introduced by
Franz H. Mautner and Henry Hatfield

Beacon Press   Beacon Hill   Boston

To

HEDI and JANE

Contents

Preface

The preface could be entitled "Lightning Rod," Lichtenberg remarks in one of his aphorisms. It may, we hope, avert some critical thunderbolts to state the limits of our intentions and the nature of our method of translating. We present here some few hundreds of his thousands of aphorisms, fewer than thirty of the more than 800 letters which have been preserved, and a very few essays.

In translating we have tried to be as faithful as possible without being unidiomatic. Where Lichtenberg's prose is smooth, polished, and "literary," we have tried to preserve those qualities in English. Where it is irregular, inelegant, showing signs of haste, we have not "improved" it, except on rare occasions when changes seemed necessary to avoid obscurity or serious infelicity. On the other hand, we have not hesitated to break up long paragraphs in the letters and essays, for the reader's convenience. Occasionally, too, a very long sentence has been replaced by two short ones: generally we have been freer in making omissions in the longer prose pieces than in the aphorisms, though a few of the latter are long enough to belie their name.

Since this is a Lichtenberg *Reader,* not an edition, we have occasionally supplied a word without using square brackets or changed a tense without defending ourselves for taking these liberties. We have not hesitated to modify punctuation in the interests of clarity. Lichtenberg's own footnotes are marked with daggers; ours with asterisks.

We are grateful to the Swarthmore College Faculty Research Fund for financing the preparation of the final draft, and to Jane Hatfield for doing most of the typing of the earlier versions. Also we must thank Edward Darling and especially

ix

Alan Levensohn of the Beacon Press for editorial guidance, and Hedi Mautner, Thomas Bledsoe, and Egon Schwarz for assistance and encouragement. We acknowledge the kind permission of the Oxford University Press to reprint the translation of Lichtenberg's passage on Garrick as Hamlet from Mare and Quarrel's *Lichtenberg's Visits to England*. For permission to reproduce the caricature of Lichtenberg we are indebted to the Joint Library of the State of Lower Saxony and the University of Göttingen.

Mr. Mautner wrote the introduction; Mr. Hatfield is primarily responsible for the translations which make up the rest of the book. But we have criticized each other's efforts frankly; many a passage as it now stands is the result of long discussion. Indeed, even in the most harmonious collaboration, as in the happiest marriage, there are elements of divergence. We hope that our occasional tensions, as well as our usual agreements, have been productive.

H. H.

F. H. M.

INTRODUCTION:

Georg Christoph Lichtenberg

I

Cultured travelers of the 1780's and '90's who passed
through the German university town of Göttingen took
pains to see one of its most noteworthy sights: the lectures in experimental physics given by Professor Georg
Christoph Lichtenberg. The lecture room, which was
in the professor's home, as was then the custom, was
crowded with students and visitors — intellectuals,
princes, dignitaries. At the proper time, the door of
the adjoining living room opened, and a little hunch-
back entered, laid his textbook and a large pocket
watch on the table in front of him, and gazed at his
listeners with dark, thoughtful eyes. Then, with a
little smile on his lips, he began his lecture: a lecture
which, though elementary in content, touched on the
most recent theories and discoveries and was sometimes
comprehensible only to a small part of his audience. But
what urbane intelligence and charm, what philosophical
sense and humor were evident! With picturesque com-
parisons he sought to make clear the most abstract problems. Often departing from the specific topic at hand,
he turned to more general questions of research and scientific method; to the history and future of man; and
to the paradoxes of man's thought and behavior. Even
when Lichtenberg spoke of Newton or Kepler (one of
his students reports in his memoirs), the smile rarely left
his lips, and this confused the simpler among the students. But there were rewarding moments for them too.
Striking experiments, in which lightning crackled and
flashed, amazed and delighted them; and the learned
professor himself was as pleased by this show as a child.

He repeatedly reminded them that all theories of natural science are only tentative — hypotheses — "myths of the physicist."

To the tradesmen and folk of the town also, Lichtenberg was a popular figure. While he was still a young man, the famous magician Philadelphus Philadelphia began to perform in Göttingen. Lichtenberg, in order to salvage the intellectual honor of the town's residents, had printed a sarcastic handbill ridiculing magic, and distributed it during the night. Later, when already a respected professor, he repeated on a hill near the town the famous new Franklin experiment, making a kite rise into the electrically charged air in order to attract lightning from the clouds. The kite tore itself free and flew to the town money lender's attic window, and the whole affair became a joyous street riot. Often Göttingen residents, passing by Lichtenberg's house, could hear the bangs of explosions inside — for this was the era of the popular experiments with the new "types of air," hydrogen and oxygen. They would nod to each other: "The professor is shooting."

Yet Lichtenberg was no seeker of popularity. He despised cheap fame, avoided parties, and rarely even visited his friends. For hours one could see him standing silent at his window, observing the people, listening to the scraps of their conversation and their shouts, following the drift of the clouds or gazing into space — thinking. This was his favorite pastime. In his later years, sadness lay often on his face. Much of what went on in the mind of this strange man on such occasions, he wrote down; a small selection of his thought is offered in this book.

II

To the historian of ideas Lichtenberg is an immensely interesting and a bewildering figure. His temperament and thought show the seemingly contradictory trends of the second part of the eighteenth century: religious inwardness and rigorous analytical rationalism, a hunger for facts and Romantic fancy. To the reader he appears timeless — a penetrating observer of man, a brilliant thinker, and a puckish humorist. Goethe described Lichtenberg's writings as "the most amazing divining rod; wherever he makes a joke, a problem is hidden." They meant much to Kierkegaard; he devoted enthusiastic thanks to the "voice in the wilderness" and used one of his "jokes" as a motto. Freud quotes them frequently. In every generation during the last 150 years, some admirer has found Lichtenberg amazingly "modern," gifted with a presentiment of the thought or the findings of his own time. Recently the noted philosopher, Isaiah Berlin, has noticed in one of Lichtenberg's aphorisms the succinct formulation of "analysis," the trend which now dominates British philosophy, and called it "certainly one of the most original remarks ever made about philosophy." Lichtenberg has also anticipated basic ideas of logical positivism or empiricism, the other important school of thought which has dominated philosophy in the Anglo-Saxon countries during this century. The revolutionary thinker Wittgenstein, who seems to have inspired them both, esteemed Lichtenberg highly; the resemblance between some of his statements and those of Lichtenberg is astounding. Nietzsche named Lichtenberg's *Aphorisms* as one of the four German prose works which alone, aside from Goethe's, deserve to be read over and over again. However, for a long time Lichtenberg's casual — or seemingly casual — observations remained gems cherished by only a small elite.

The slow spread of Lichtenberg's fame began to accelerate around the beginning of this century and has become rapid during the last two decades. In France and Germany, his humane, cosmopolitan outlook and his graceful wit served as a relief from the spirit of the Nazi period. Despite his easy manner, existentialists found in his thoughts, in his suspicion of rigid intellectual systems, something like their own doubts and anxieties, their own reliance on the self. Today, Lichtenberg is being read in the German-speaking countries in a host of editions and has been translated into most European languages. He is frequently ranked above that other great moralist, La Rochefoucauld, for the scope and the depth of his thinking and the subtlety of his imagery. Yet he is still a stranger in the world of English letters.

Who was Lichtenberg? He was born in 1742. His father, a talented clergyman, died when the boy was nine years old. The impoverished widow somehow managed to send his two older brothers to the university, but he had to wait until the age of twenty-one, when a scholarship enabled him to enroll at the University of Göttingen to study philosophy, mathematics, and natural science. This school — founded less than thirty years earlier under the sponsorship of Hanover's ruler, King George II of England — was the most modern and liberal of the German universities. When Lichtenberg arrived, it had already become one of the best known seats of learning in Europe. He impressed his teachers so much by the excellence and originality of his mind, by the energy with which he threw himself into studies in many fields, and by his practical skills — of great importance at that time for an experimental scientist — that he was offered two professorships soon after he had left the university. One of the calls, from Göttingen, reached him in England, where he had gone for a few months "to prepare himself better for his duties." He returned to Göttingen in 1770 as Professor of Mathematics and Astronomy, went to England once more in 1774, stayed there for sixteen months, and then remained in Göttingen until his death in 1799.

The story of his career and fame is strange and paradoxical. He was considered an eminent figure among the European scientists of his day, and was known for his brilliance as a teacher, the first in Germany to use experiments extensively. He was at home in most fields of science — he saw them as an inseparable whole — and treated his chosen subjects incisively, yet with a bold philosophical outlook. An adventurous imagination was balanced by great circumspection in his methods and by a radical skepticism. The adventures of his imagination sprang from his temperament; he clung to skepticism from conviction. He constantly searched for chances to use the findings of science for the improvement of society. The most famous physicists and astronomers of his time — and the greatest minds of Germany, Goethe and Kant — admired him and had cordial relations with him. Herschel came to Göttingen to visit Lichtenberg; Volta stayed in his house and they experimented together. He was made a member of the great European academies — London, Petersburg, Leyden. Yet today the scientist Lichtenberg is hardly known. It was his mind and his method, not any outstanding findings, that made his reputation. The hopes aroused by his discovery of "electric figures" — still named after him in our textbooks of physics — which were expected

to help clarify the nature of electricity, were not fulfilled. (He found that positive electricity conducted
through metal plates covered with a powder could
produce certain figures different from those caused by
negative current. Only in recent years have scientists
begun to understand and use them.) With the progress
of physics and the establishment of a new chemistry in
the first decades of the nineteenth century, his name
faded from the consciousness of the scientists.

The opposite happened with Lichtenberg, the man
of letters. He became known to the educated as the
author of the widely-read *Göttinger Taschen-Kalender*
(Pocket Almanac). For more than twenty years he wrote
for this little almanac short essays, *causeries,* and brief
notes in such diverse fields as the arts and belles-lettres,
physics, astronomy, chemistry, technology, anthropology,
and women's fashions — mostly insignificant little items,
destined to be read once and forgotten forever. Some
of these essays attracted the attention of the keenest
and most sophisticated minds in Germany. They noticed the enlightened, humane attitude expressed in the
almanac and in a few of his pamphlets and were delighted by the witty and philosophical manner in which
they were written. Startling remarks here and there, the
ironical yet graceful use of a connotation, showed a
superior intelligence and radically independent thinking. In the first volumes his arguments and satire were
most often directed against the cult of unrestrained
emotionalism then fashionable in German life and letters.

Lichtenberg's two visits to England confirmed his
own outlook and determined his attitude for the next
ten or twenty years. He had always felt a distaste for
provincial narrow-mindedness, for the pomposity and
quarrelsome pedantry of so many German professors, and

for the commoners' meekness before an aristocracy which was often uneducated, heartless, and arrogant. In England he met enlightened noblemen and scholars who were men of the world; he spent many afternoons and evenings with the King and his family as their respected guest and friend. He felt like a new-born man in London, where he was breathing the air of an empire, not of a parish. In the streets and in the port, in the theaters and inns of London, and in the gardens of Kew, he experienced life on a larger scale and of a new richness. He admired the freedom of political and religious expression, and particularly English education, which was made to form men of action and thought, not of learning and obedience:

If I want to have some fun, I imagine one of our fifteen-year-old learned youths in the company of a fifteen-year-old English boy who's returning from Eton. The first with his hair tied up in a wig, powdered, humble and tensely anxious to let fly with a lot of learning at the slightest provocation; in his opinions merely a small-scale, inferior copy of his papa or tutor. The English boy, his clean, curly hair hanging over his ears and forehead, his face glowing, his hands all scratched, with a cut on each knuckle; Horace, Homer, and Virgil are always present in his mind; he is definite and original in his opinions, makes a thousand mistakes, but always corrects himself, etc.

On his return to Germany he felt as if in exile, in spite or because of the academic atmosphere of Göttingen. For a time he turned away from the philosophical ideal which mirrored his own type of intelligence: subtle, undogmatic thinking, analyzed in accordance with abstract principles. Now he praised common sense — which he considered characteristically English — as the greatest virtue of the mind. While he soon returned to a more balanced view of those two patterns of thought, England remained his Paradise Lost for the rest of his life.

Lichtenberg's second stay in England brought out some of his best literary gifts. In his *Letters from England,* which appeared in 1776 and 1778, he delighted his readers by his unusual power to bring close to them the atmosphere of the English stage, its personalities, their gestures and facial expressions, their speech and their costumes. Lichtenberg's description, for example, of Garrick as Hamlet, encountering his father's ghost — factual even where it depicts the terrifying — is one of the model pieces of German prose, a stock in trade of German school anthologies:

Hamlet appears in a black dress, the only one in the whole court, alas! still worn for his poor father, who has been dead scarce a couple of months. Horatio and Marcellus, in uniform, are with him, and they are awaiting the ghost; Hamlet has folded his arms under his cloak and pulled his hat down over his eyes; it is a cold night and just twelve o'clock. The theater is darkened, and the whole audience of some thousands are as quiet, and their faces as motionless, as though they were painted on the walls of the theater; even from the farthest end of the playhouse one could hear a pin drop. Suddenly, as Hamlet moves towards the back of the stage slightly to the left and turns his back on the audience, Horatio starts and, saying, "Look, my lord, it comes," points to the right, where the ghost has already appeared and stands motionless, before any one is aware of him.

At these words Garrick turns sharply and at the same moment staggers back two or three paces with his knees giving away under him; his hat falls to the ground, and both his arms, especially the left, are *stretched out nearly to their full length, with the hands as high as his head, the right arm more bent and the hand lower, and the fingers apart; his mouth is open: thus he stands rooted to the spot, with legs apart, but no loss of dignity, supported by his friends, who are better acquainted with the apparition and fear lest he should collapse. His whole demeanor is so expressive of terror that it made my flesh creep even before he began to speak. The almost terror-struck silence of the audience, which preceded this appearance and filled one with a sense of insecurity, probably did much to enhance this effect. At last he speaks, not at the beginning, but at the end of a breath, with a trembling voice: "Angels and ministers of grace defend us!" words which supply anything this scene may lack and make it one of the greatest and most terrible which will ever be played on any stage. The ghost beckons to him; I wish you could see him, with eyes fixed on the ghost, though he is speaking to his companions, freeing himself from their restraining hands, as they warn him not to follow and hold him back.**

To watch, to describe, and to interpret Garrick's performance meant more to Lichtenberg than mere interest in a great actor. Human nature, and the human body as a medium of expressing it, had always fascinated him; they were favorite subjects of his diary notes. To Lichtenberg, Garrick was one of three Englishmen — Hogarth and Shakespeare were the others — who knew the dark regions of man's nature better than any Germans and depicted human peculiarities and absurdities with the greatest effectiveness.

The article "Against Physiognomics" was Lichtenberg's main contribution to his almanac for 1778. Phys-

* Translated in Margaret L. Mare and W. H. Quarrel, *Lichtenberg's Visits to England* (Oxford, 1938), pp. 9–10.

iognomics, thought to be an intuitive skill which would develop into the science of reading a man's soul in his face, was the rage of the day. Scientists, philosophers, and religious apostles alike were convinced that the spirit must manifest itself in the flesh. Cutting silhouettes was the vogue. What Lichtenberg had to say about this problem deserved special attention, for it came from a man whose letters on the English theater effectively described the body as an expression of the soul, from a man who confessed that his "chief concern" since the days of his childhood had been to observe people's faces. But in this essay he demolished the physiognomic theories and divested the interpretation of a man's physical features of all scientific claims, metaphysics, and sentimentality. The only things that are sometimes significant, he found, are facial gestures which through frequent repetition may become permanent traits. Lichtenberg discussed his theory so intelligently, with so much detailed concreteness, warmth, and wit, that it caused a great stir. The article was reprinted as a booklet and established Lichtenberg's reputation as a writer, which grew in the following years through his satirical pamphlets and the essays and narrative fantasies in his almanac. Moreover Lichtenberg was known to the most educated among German readers as editor of a rather scholarly journal, the *Göttingisches Magazin*.

Lichtenberg became famous through his *Explanations of Hogarth's Engravings*. These appeared for years — first as brief comments in his *Pocket Almanac*; then, from 1794 until his death, in more extensive form as a separate publication. In these learned yet lively discussions, he applied to Hogarth's dramatic scenes his knowledge of England and the English and a concept of physiognomy which was bold and comprehensive, but down-to-earth. "Physiognomy" now meant to him, in addition to "frozen" facial gestures, the

sum of all the visible manifestations of personality — a
man's gait, his clothing and his manner of wearing it,
the furniture in his house — in short, his entire appearance and material environment, as far as it is subject to his will, his temperament, and his impulses.
These symptoms are precisely the means which Hogarth
ingeniously used to characterize his figures. Since,
furthermore, Lichtenberg found in Hogarth an unusually vast and subtle knowledge of human nature, "explanations" of these pictures provided him with an opportunity to convey in casual side-remarks his own
psychological insights. Goethe reports in his autobiography that the *Explanations* "created the greatest sensation."

When Lichtenberg died in 1799, he was eulogized
as one of Germany's best essayists and satirists and as her
wittiest writer. He had stood outside the great renas-
cence of the German mind in the last quarter of the
century which had produced Goethe and Schiller. He
had been sarcastic at first, when it started as radical
emotionalism, and silent later, when it became the "clas-
sical movement." He had not accomplished any work in
the genres in which a literary man had to excel to be
considered great — poetry, drama, the novel — and he
might well have been forgotten gradually by all but the
historians of literature, had not something happened
that caused a new turn in the story of his renown.

III

Shortly after Lichtenberg's death, his publisher an-
nounced an edition of some of his literary remains.
One section would especially appeal to Lichtenberg's

friends, "although it contains fragments only." Actually, these "fragments" were but a small selection from the work which was to become better known than anything else Lichtenberg had written, and for which alone he is widely known today — his books of aphorisms. These he himself would have hardly called a "work." They were culled from sixteen notebooks whose purpose Lichtenberg once described:

The merchants have their Waste Book;* *there they record from day to day everything they buy and sell, one after the other, without any order. From there the entries go into the* Journal * *where everything is recorded more systematically, and finally it goes to the* Ledger at Double Entrance.* *This should be imitated by the scholars. First a book in which I write everything the way I see it or as my thinking tells me to. Then this can be copied into another where subjects are separated and arranged in better order; and the* Ledger *could then contain the various subjects in their connection and, following from it, their proper discussion.*

There were hundreds of remarks in each of these "waste books," ranging in size from pregnant one-word hints to whole paragraphs. Lichtenberg had entered them almost every day — in later years, he added the date — whenever the mood came upon him as he read and reflected, day-dreamed, or observed. Some consisted merely in effective or amusing phrases; some were worded with great precision in carefully balanced form; others he had obviously jotted down on the spur of the moment and left for later thinking over or reshaping, or for mere experimentation. For he believed, like Valéry in our century, that a trying out of ideas, similar to the methods of the experimental scientist, might lead to some fruitful thought or discovery. *I have the habit,* he wrote

---

* Lichtenberg gives these terms in English.

in one of his letters, *of putting down my ideas about all
kinds of things, by no means in order to use them at
some later time, but simply with the intention of trying out their connection with each other. For in writing down things, one notices a great deal which one
is not aware of in mere meditation.* This motive for Lichtenberg's use of the aphoristic method is obviously quite
different from the one mentioned above. Actually, they
do not exclude each other: they simply indicate different aspects of the fact that thinking in aphorisms was
natural to him.

These notes dealt with everything that might strike
an alert mind as worthy of reflection and with some
facts that had never before been thought of as strange
or problematic. Some of the more traditional questions
around which his thinking circled were the relationship of body and mind, of reason and feeling, of language and thought, of man and woman, of idea and
reality. Some others were startlingly new, anticipations
of twentieth century depth psychology: Do dreams not
have something to do with one's character, great achievements with feelings of inferiority? Is not a young man's
impulse to write books a disguised effect of the sexual
drive? What happens in the mind when, looking at a
number of meaningless and unrelated single objects on
the wallpaper, it shapes a form, a *Gestalt?* God, virtues
and vices, a man's face, the history of the earth, politics,
poets, peasants, individual style, national character, the
speech of the servants, falling in love, making love, being
in love — he approached all his subjects with freshness
of thought and observation. He experienced the child's
delights in discovery, and presented his findings now
with the seriousness of the philosopher, now with brilliant sarcasm or with tongue in cheek.

His notes are sometimes the results of long reflections, crystallized in one short statement or question, and sometimes sudden flashes of insight, light thrown into the depth of the human unconscious. For most of these thousands of entries have ultimately one theme — man. Lichtenberg's own intellectual temperament and the tendencies of his era coincide in this interest. Physically impaired since childhood, he looked at life as an outsider. Observing it intensely and feeling deeply, he was forced to reflect about man and his behavior, and he lived in a century which favored such reflection.

Lichtenberg believed he could best understand, unprejudiced by dogmas and inveterate theories, what is essential in the "real" man, by knowing more about his soul: *There is nothing about which I would like more to read the secret opinions of thinking men than about the subject of the soul. I'm not interested in the loudly publicized ones; these I know already. These do not belong to psychology but rather to a collection of statutes.* He found rich material, more useful than those publicized opinions, in watching the soul in its least observed functions, its oddities and errors — slips of the tongue and of the mind. To notice them amused him enormously. He could have written Boswell's remark, "I have regretted that there is no invention for getting an immediate and exact transcript of the mind, like that instrument by which a copy of a letter is at once taken off." He was equally entertained by the next best means to advance from academic theories about the soul to its reality, observations of the peculiarities of individual persons, including himself.

The third noteworthy aspect of the human soul, in addition to its nature and its individual peculiarities, was for him the process of thinking — the formation of concepts and ideas. Just as he considered the most trivial functions of the mind not self-evident, but objects for observation and sources of amused surprise, so he considered thinking not merely a tool, but a subject for investigation — and along with thinking, its medium, language.

Lichtenberg's ideas sometimes contradict each other, but the reader soon becomes aware of a distinctly personal inner unity behind the contradictions of his aphorisms — his "system of thoughts," he called it. This should be sufficient reason not to look primarily for Lichtenberg's "opinions." He shared opinions with many, the intensity of his thought and the originality of his mind with none. If we disregard his involvement in literary questions of the day, and his contempt for pompous mediocrity, we might say that almost his only inflexible attitude is his passionate respect for the dignity of every human being. He expressed it very simply in one of his letters: *I have a very high concept of the greatness and dignity of man.* From this credo derives his equally passionate conviction that a part of this dignity is the right and the duty of every man to think for himself, not blindly to accept a doctrine, a system, a belief: *Since, once and for all, we have seats in God's House of Commons, and He Himself has entrusted us with the vote, shall we not express our opinion?*

We find scores of these appeals to himself in Lichtenberg's notebooks; more important, he carried them out. His tenets turned into an attitude and a quality of his mind. It is for this reason that Schopenhauer called him one of the few "philosophers" who deserve this name — the original thinkers who care for truth and nothing else. *To doubt things which are now believed without any further investigation whatsoever, that's the main point everywhere,* Lichtenberg ad-

monished himself in 1793, when the fever of the En-
lightenment had generally calmed down in Europe,
twenty-three years after that outburst of his own youthful
intellectual enthusiasm. Yet this skepticism incited him
to constructive thought, to ever renewed checking and
investigation: *Before anything else, extension of the
frontiers of learning. Without this, all is in vain.*

Lichtenberg's thinking was subtle and profound,
and for this very reason he understood that thinking
is not the only nor always the ultimate means of knowing. As a scientist he also knew that the choice of
instruments determines the kind of results. Was not
human reason merely *one* kind of instrument? While
he was determined not to accept any established belief
or doctrine without rational and empirical examination,
this examination itself became an investigation of the
very doctrines of both reason and appearance as the
ultimate sources of knowledge. Can either of these be
in fact applied to all subjects and experiences? Such
questions underlie all his observations of things and
people, of institutions and theories, and make them vi-
brant with curiosity, meaningful beyond themselves.

Intuition, for example, should not be disregarded
even in science: *Everything has its depths. He who
has eyes, sees everything in everything.* And: *Wit is
the discoverer and reason the observer.* He admired the
power of instinct in life and in nature; he had himself discovered impressive examples of the forces of the
unconscious: *I commend dreams again; we live and feel
as much dreaming as waking and are the one as much
as the other. It is one of the superiorities of man that
he dreams, and knows it. We have hardly made the
right use of this yet. Dream is a life which, combined with the rest of us, makes up what we call human
life. Dreams gradually merge into our waking; we*

cannot say where man's waking state begins. Or again: *I believe that instinct in man anticipates discursive reasoning and that therefore men of minor learning but exact perception have discovered many a matter which discursive reasoning cannot, as of now, attain and pursue.* In a bold reversal of the usual arguments, he sees in the conviction of free will, with which we flatter ourselves, nothing but instinctive subordination to necessity. *Salt which crystallizes does God's will (or whatever everybody may, and in the end must, call God). It does His will and doesn't know it; man does it with a feeling which he calls consciousness and — this means even more — with the feeling he would have been able* not *to fulfill that will, if he only wanted to.*

Thinking must clarify, but not replace reality. Lichtenberg demanded of science and literature "things, not words," but he yielded willingly to overwhelming emotions. One of his earliest convictions was that life, being a whole, must be lived by the whole man: *The whole man must move together* was the motto of one of his diaries. He asserted this belief over and over again: *Now reason stands out above the realm of the obscure but warm emotions like the Alpine peaks above the clouds. They see the sun more clearly and more distinctly, but they are cold and sterile.* Such thoughts protected him in good times from allowing his analyzing reason too much power over his daily life, but they did not prevent his thinking from energetically pushing on to the question: How much "reality" has the world which is perceived by our senses, and how much truth is there in our conclusions about it? Stronger or new instruments will reveal objects and relations of whose existence we have not the slightest knowledge. And a world interpreted only in accordance with inherent qualities of our senses and of our thinking, patterned by our language, is not *the* world. It is only one of many possible worlds.

Some of Lichtenberg's gradually evolving ideas are excitingly close to the solutions of philosophical problems which have been attempted in this century through the application of "linguistic analysis" to the "positivistic" approach, yet they are practically unknown to most Anglo-Saxon practitioners of this method. Lichtenberg's philosophical thinking had started from Leibniz, proceeded through and past Hume's writings, and had, when Kant's main works appeared, come more than half-way towards their central ideas. Lichtenberg studied Kant with excitement and mostly enthusiastic approval, but he preserved his own intellectual independence. His own philosophical reservations remained the theoretical framework for everything he did, said, taught. The textbook on physics he was planning might well start out, he wrote, by showing that everything we sense and think is mere consciousness of the modifications of our self. It should also stress the crudeness and the fragmentary character of our knowledge, and he admonished himself: *Do not use the word "hypothesis," even less "theory," but "mode of imagining."*

Thoughts like these, his enjoyment of the experimental method, and his enthusiasm at the power of human thought to force the mysterious phenomena of the physical world into a logically consistent "mode of imagining," may have produced the smile which often accompanied Lichtenberg's lectures. He never forgot that our thinking has become petrified in words. Words originally were images, but are now frozen into concepts; these, in turn, are connected with each other in ways not separable from our grammar. In speaking and listening we live in a "world of words," yet this kind of thinking pretends to reproduce "reality"! *I and me. I*

*feel me — that makes two objects. Our false philosophy
is embodied in the language as a whole: one might say
that we can't reason without reasoning wrongly. People
don't bear in mind that speaking, no matter about what,
is a philosophy. Everyone who speaks is a folk-philosopher,
and our academic philosophy consists of qualifications of
the popular brand. All our philosophy is an improving of
linguistic usage; that is, an improving of a philosophy —
of the most common of all, in fact. But the ordinary philosophy has the advantage of possessing the declensions
and conjugations. Thus we always teach true philosophy
in the language of the false one. Defining words is no
help; for by using such explanations, I don't change
the pronouns and their declensions.* Such considera-
tions throw light upon Lichtenberg's distrust of all
rigid intellectual systems and upon his belief in the
aphoristic method of finding truth, his "experimenting
with ideas." They also support his innate love of the
metaphor: *When we use an old word, it will often stay
in the groove of meaning dug by the primer, but a
metaphor makes a new groove and often cuts straight
through.*

Lichtenberg may also have been inclined to laugh-
ter when, absorbed in the most earnest speculations, he
tried to disengage his own thinking about man and the
universe from the traditional patterns of thought. The
metaphor with its extended analogies was one simple
means; to *look into the telescope at the wrong end*
seemed perhaps the simplest way of arriving at a new
view. And he could think of many other possible per-
spectives, which together would lead to the conviction
that *strange things are indeed happening among us
Earthlanders.* Lichtenberg's scientific knowledge merged
with his day-dreams, and his critical reasoning with his
capricious imagination, to produce strange aphorisms

which tend to look merely bizarre. Yet theoretical thoughts are embodied there, often with a flavor of satire or as a kind of new mythology: *We, the tail of the world, don't know what its head is planning.* And: *Humans write much about the essence of matter. I wish matter would some day start writing about the human soul. It would become clear that up to now we have been far from really understanding each other.*

But his awareness of the limitations of reason did not always result in jokes, daydreams, smiles, or renewed striving for truth. On bad days, during periods of pathological depression in his later life, awareness turned into despair: *Since the middle of the year 1791, something that I can't really describe as yet has been stirring the whole economy of my thoughts. It is an extraordinary distrust of all human knowledge, except for mathematics, and the only thing which still ties me to the study of physics is the hope of finding out something useful to mankind.* Yet even in mathematics he would not exclude doubts about the most elementary statements. Euclid's *Elements of Geometry* are based on axioms derived from common sense; Lichtenberg was in no way sure that they might not be refuted or qualified some day. He entrusted to his notebooks even his doubts whether the law of causality not be merely an idea, not a reality—a thought which finds much support in present-day mathematics, physics, and philosophy. Shortly before his death, Lichtenberg wrote: *To reduce everything in man to simple principles means in the end, it seems, that we assume there must be such a* principium — *and how can this be proved?*

Despite this radical skepticism and relativism, Lichtenberg considered common sense the most valuable intellectual quality in man. In many entries he made fun of the scholar who lacked it: *This man was so intelligent*

that he could not be used for anything in the world.
His ideal was *the healthy scholar, the man in whom
thinking is not a disease.* Moreover, some day greater
knowledge or more advanced science may show the
truth of superstitions smiled at today by the intellectual:
There is a great difference between still *believing something and believing it* again. Still *to believe that the
moon affects the plants reveals stupidity and superstition, but to believe it* again *is a sign of philosophy
and reflection.*

Lichtenberg decided, with his respect for the
practical, that the context and purpose of each question
must determine the method we should employ in the
search for an answer. In daily life and everyday science,
we should trust our senses: *Common sense is, in my
opinion, at a very respectable point on the ladder of
our knowledge, so that it could very well be used as a
starting point. It is not the starting point of ladders
which is under discussion, but "Where must I start in
1790 in order to secure the greatest possible benefit?"*
We must not underestimate the wisdom of the heart:
*Is reason, or rather the intellect, really better off when
it arrives at final causes than when it arrives at a
command of the heart? After all, it is surely a very
open question which ties us more strongly to the world
surrounding us, the heart or reason.* We should believe
our feelings, trust God ("whatever He is") in misery
and be thankful to Him in happiness, yet be aware that
neither our sense perceptions nor our belief in God can
be seen as "truth" outside the categories of human
thinking. *Man has not the power to shape the world
according to his wishes, but he has the power to grind
eye-glasses through which he can make it appear almost according to his wishes.* This knowledge need
not intrude on our devotion, but can increase it. For

the view which appealed most to Lichtenberg on scientific, logical, and emotional grounds was Spinoza's pantheism — the belief in the identity of God with the laws of nature embodied in Nature, and with man as part of it. He was aware that this monistic concept cannot exist outside the forms of human thinking; contemplation of this very thought could stir him with the depth and force of religious feeling. *Amintor's Morning Prayer* is a moving document of this attitude. The religion he considered best for the non-philosopher was Christianity. The purposeful existence of man's belief in God seemed more important to him than the question of God's own existence: *Is it really so absolutely certain that our reason can know nothing metaphysical? Might man not be able to weave his ideas of God with just as much purpose as the spider weaves his net to catch flies? Or, in other words: might not beings exist who admire us as much for our ideas of God and immortality as we admire the spider and the silkworm?*

IV

It is surprising that a man whose most eminent gift seems to be deep thought, a writer whom we find absorbed again and again in daydreams and reflection about himself, should at the same time be a startlingly successful observer of the world around him. Lichtenberg sees more than others, more detail and more meaning. To be sure, this keenness of vision and immediate understanding are parts of his natural endowment, but his intuitions are confirmed by his basic theoretical idea, that of wholeness and unity in the world of things and of man. *Everything is identical with itself, each part represents the whole. I have sometimes seen my entire life in an hour.* Even as a student, he criticized contemporary philosophy for seeing a person's character *not as a very neatly constructed totality* and for regarding emotions *as adhesive beauty patches, which we may shift or throw away at will.* The same holds true for his appearance.

To "look" — especially at man — was sheer joy for him: *Once in Hanover my apartment was so located that my window opened onto a narrow street which connected two large ones. It was very pleasant to see how people's faces changed when they came into the small street where they thought they were less noticed, how one man was pissing while another one over there was tying his stocking, one was laughing up his sleeve and still another shook his head. Some girls thought smilingly of the past night and arranged their ribbons for conquests in the next large street.*

Nothing special need happen: *To me the most entertaining surface on the earth is the human face.* He recalls: *I once saw in Stade such peacefulness combined with a furtive smile — in the face of a fellow who had succeeded in driving his swine into a bathing place which they usually disliked entering — as I have never seen since.* That smile, furtive and peaceful, told him in a flash much about the fellow's inner constitution and perhaps his place in society. Lichtenberg was also alert to record his own feelings on the threshold of consciousness, which seemed to him part of our understanding of man: *Who has never felt throughout his whole being a hat with a lopsided brim which he had to wear, or felt an awkward cane-knob in his arm?*

Lichtenberg used observation and intuition judiciously. He saw the springs that make a person act and their connections, and laid them bare. To the perceptive descriptions and interpretations of human behavior by the great moralists who preceded him — Theophrastus, Montaigne, La Bruyère, and La Rochefoucauld — he added refinements and discoveries of his own. Nietzsche owed him a great deal; the neo-pragmatists of this century have used his psychological observations to support their philosophical doctrines.

Lichtenberg's imagination not only goes deep, it also spreads wide, thanks to the vastness of the material ever-present in his mind. "A world of relationships was at his mind's disposal," Goethe remarked, "to be shuffled like playing cards and to be dealt with roguishly at his pleasure." His eye and ear and mind are always open to mental associations; he senses them everywhere. Evoked by situations and concepts, by phrases and words, even by sounds, they result in surprising analogies and fanciful conclusions, stated seriously or tongue in cheek. Lichtenberg cultivated this "making of canals" between remote areas in adherence to the eighteenth-century theories about the essence of wit. Sometimes this habit may deteriorate into a mannerism, yet often it brings into play his spontaneous fantasy, which roams from man to angels and plants, from God to crystals and beasts. Lichtenberg is one of the few writers in whom lucidity joins with the bizarre; sarcasm and wit blend with the smiling humor which understands all that troubles the race, confuses it, and makes it behave a little foolishly.

This detachment, together with his playfulness (which extends to words as much as to thoughts) produces much of the atmosphere of hilarity so characteristic of long stretches of Lichtenberg's writings. His facility with words, the obvious pleasure he takes in a well-coined phrase, contribute to it enormously; the reader shares his enjoyment at capturing in picturesque comparison the bearing of a man among his fellow men. *He moved as slowly as an hour-hand amidst a crowd of second-hands.* Or his intellectual make-up: *When he was expected to use his mind, he felt like a right-handed person who has to do something with his left.* Or: *He swallowed a lot of wisdom, but it seemed as if all of it had gone down the wrong way.* Human warmth can be diffused in a physiognomic one-sentence sketch: *He was standing there as sadly as the little drinking cup of a bird who has been dead for some time.* And satire in two words: *An Amen-face.*

In general, Lichtenberg's manner of writing reflects his intellectual characteristics: in his many qualifying clauses, his precise, cautious thinking; in his many questions, his pondering about accepted dogmas; and in his statements of facts, bare of all comment, his smile at the paradoxical aspects of human thought and action. One should therefore not be too ready to shake one's head over some of Lichtenberg's seemingly banal remarks: it is precisely the banal which often strikes him as mysterious or funny or moving. (We might be aware of his warning, *When a book and a head collide and there is a hollow sound, is it always in the book?*) What a world of thoughts is awakened by the brief sentence: *And there sat the great man watching his little kittens!* It is in the nature of the aphorism to let the reader reflect himself, and the aphoristic style is Lichtenberg's ideal: *When people can no longer hear a man thinking, he must speak. As soon as he reaches the point where he can again presuppose thoughts of the same nature as his, he must stop speaking. Most books contain nothing between two interesting points but the most ordinary common sense: a heavily drawn line where a dotted one would have sufficed.* And again: *The writer who can't at times throw away a thought about which another would have written dissertations, unworried whether or not the reader will find it, will never become a great writer.* After all, in most instances, his notes do not aim at any reader, but are records of his conversations with himself; sometimes he adds: *I understand myself.*

Where he writes for publication, and where he does not feel he has to joke, his style transposes into language the ideal of man he had set up for the Germans. He strives for factualness and simplicity, for clarity without pedantry; he prefers understatement to solemnity, and avoids pompousness like a disease. He wants to write as a man of the world. (He had gone to England, he once wrote, in order to learn how to write German.) Conciseness is the mark of both the man of the world and the healthy thinker. Once he chides himself: *In this expression the thought has too much play; I pointed with the head of a cane where I should have pointed with the tip of a needle.* His images, puns, and word creations serve him as means of abridged talking; he adopts Pope's term, "nevergreen," as the key word of the melancholy aphorism: *The paths are bordered with nevergreen.*

There is much elegance of construction in his writing. The satirist, almost by definition, thinks in antitheses — *They feel with their heads and think with their hearts* — and the mathematician in Lichtenberg often expresses himself in precise formulas and equations. Yet, like that other religious scientist-aphorist, Pascal, Lichtenberg declares himself against "false windows for the sake of symmetry." Where a problem is intricate or where a statement should be qualified, his intellectual conscientiousness does not permit him oversimplification, however pleasing it might be aesthetically. (Formal balance and aesthetic perfection at the cost of intellectual honesty seemed to him the sin of some overly-praised French writing and of French science.) Thus his notes have many more qualifiers — "perhaps," "sometimes," "mostly" — and question marks than the fine architectural precision of La Rochefoucauld's maxims would permit. On the other hand, pedantry must not kill wit pregnant with truth: *The great sleight-of-hand trick of taking small deviations from the truth for truth itself — a trick on which the whole differential calculus is built — is also the basis of our ingenious thoughts. They would often collapse if we were to regard the deviations with philosophical severity.*

V

So much about Lichtenberg's work — about the professor, the thinker, the writer. What of the man himself?

Physically, he was marked by his small stature and the big hump on his back. He was sometimes embarrassed by it, and shy in large company, but it did not make him miserable. He did not care much for acquaintances, but valued immensely the friendship of three or four of his colleagues; on the whole, he remained an outsider. He was the kindest of men and very susceptible to good wine and the charms of the other sex. His mistresses were girls from the poorest families. He loved two of them deeply: one, Maria-Dorothea Stechard, died as a young girl; and he married the second, Margarete Kellner, his housekeeper, in order to entitle her to a pension, when, at the age of forty-seven, he thought death was coming. Göttingen society never forgave the professor this marriage, but the match made him as happy as his temperament permitted.

He was cheerful by nature, but seized by fits of melancholy, even as a young man: in his own words, he could "voluptuously enjoy" these moods when they were stirred up by a longing for his absent friends or his dead parents, by religious piety, or by the beauty and greatness of nature. On the other hand, watching tumultuous street scenes or the colorful activity in the harbors of London and Hamburg could also delight him and make him exuberantly happy. He had to struggle all his life to find an emotional balance between sharply contrasting tendencies within himself which he was able to reconcile only intellectually: deep religiosity and radical skepticism, superstition and rationality, a passion for perfection and a pathological lack of will power in his work. (He always planned to write a satirical novel, but never finished more than a few pages.) Strong sensuality never left him. In his thirties and forties, the attacks of melancholy became more frequent and more poignant through hypochrondriac attention to his physical being. He felt sick most of the time without being seriously ill, was aware of the nervous character of his ailments, and tried now and then to make fun of them in his "wastebooks."

From these, from a few volumes of even more private diaries, and from his letters we know Lichtenberg's inmost being in great detail, for he observed himself with the same detached curiosity which he used to turn upon others. He kept the promise to himself in his diary in his thirtieth year: *I am determined never to tell an untruth to this book. I'll make it a glass which shall reflect myself to myself in future times.* This purpose grew into a greater one. He planned to use these notes for what he hoped would be one of the main works of his life: his autobiography as a true panorama of an individual's soul, unprejudiced by the categories of textbook psychology: *I have worked for a long time at a history of my mind and of my wretched body, written with such sincerity that some people may feel shame for me. I want to tell it with greater sincerity than any of my readers will perhaps believe. This is a still almost untrod path to immortality. Because of the wicked world it won't appear until my death.*

A few of these entries, most of them written down between the twenty-sixth and forty-seventh years of his life, follow here:

Character of a person of my acquaintance.

His body is so constituted that even a bad draftsman working in the dark would be able to draw it better. If he had the power to change it, he would give less relief to some of its parts. This man has always been fairly satisfied with his health, although it is not of the best; he has to a high degree the gift of profiting from his good days. On such occasions his imagination, his most faithful companion, never deserts him; he stands behind the window, his head propped between his hands, and — while the passer-by sees nothing but a melancholically drooping head — he often silently confesses to himself that once again he has too much indulged in pleasure.

He has few friends; actually his heart is always open only to one friend who is present, but to several absent ones also. His friendliness makes many believe that he is their friend. He serves them out of ambition or humaneness, but in this he's not driven by that impulse which drives him to serve his real friends. He has loved only once or twice, once not unhappily, but the other time happily. He won, merely through gaiety and lightheartedness, a good soul, with the result that these now often fail him. Yet he will forever revere gaiety and lightheartedness as those qualities of his soul which procured for him the most joyful hours of his life: if he could choose a second life and another soul, I doubt whether he would choose different ones.

About religion he had very free thoughts already as a boy, but he never sought any special recognition for being a freethinker, nor for believing everything without exception. He can pray with fervor and has never been able to read the 90th psalm without an indescribable feeling of exaltation. He doesn't know which he hates more, young officers or young preachers; he wouldn't be able to live for long with either. His body and his attire have seldom been good enough for formal parties, and his convictions seldom . . .* enough. He hopes he will never have meals of more than three courses at noon and two in the evening, with some wine, nor does he ever want to be reduced to less than potatoes, apples, bread, and some wine every day. In either case he would be unhappy. Reading and writing are as necessary to him as eating and drinking, and he hopes he will never lack books. Of death he thinks often, and never with aversion; he wishes he could think of everything with the same detachment, and hopes that, when the time comes, his Creator will gently take from him a life of which he was, it is true, not a very economical, but neither a wicked owner.

I remember distinctly that, when I was quite young, I once wanted to teach a calf how to retrieve, yet although I saw at once that I was improving noticeably

* Lichtenberg's dots.

in the necessary skills, we understood one another less each day, and finally I gave up completely and have never tried again.

(Lion) ** Often finds pleasure in figuring out means of killing this or that person, or of setting fires without its being noticed. Without ever having firmly resolved to do such a thing, or having even the least inclination, he very often fell asleep thinking such thoughts. After his sixteenth year, he could no longer convince himself that Christ was God's son. This idea became so familiar to him and so much part of him that there was no more thought of trying to convince him. He regretted only that Christ Himself did not write and leave us more information about Joseph of Arimathea. He knew too well what pious fanatics can do in such a situation. His faith in the efficacy of prayer, his superstition in many respects — kneeling, touching the Bible and kissing it; downright adoration of his sainted mother.

(Lion). In his 10th year he falls in love with a boy called Schmidt (the head boy in the town school), son of a tailor. Likes to hear anything about him and induces the boys to talk about their conversations with him; has never himself spoken to him, but was very pleased to hear that the boy had spoken about him. Climbed a wall after school to watch him go home from school. Now, still remembers his features very distinctly; the boy seems to him nothing less than handsome, with a turned-up nose and red cheeks. But he was at the head of his form. I would regret it if, by admitting this freely, I should increase distrust of the world, but I was a human being. Lion knew few people

** *Lion* (in English) indicates remarks about himself.

in the world whose weakness he hadn't found out after three weeks' acquaintance (counting the hours of association only, which could well amount to three months in the calendar) and he has become convinced that no dissembling helps against an association of three weeks. Has never acted unjustly from avarice, so help me God.

Desultory reading has always been my greatest pleasure.

I must not forget that I once put the question "What are the Northern Lights?" addressed to an angel, on the floor of Graupner's attic, and next morning sneaked up there, most shyly, for the note. Oh, if only some practical joker had answered the note!

In the house where I lived, I had learned the sound and the pitch of each step of the old wooden stairs and also the time which each of my friends beat when he came to call on me. I must confess that I trembled every time I heard the stairs played upon by some pair of feet coming up in a melody unknown to me.

I know little about music and can't play any instrument — except that I can whistle well. I've derived more advantage from this than many others have from their arias on the flute and the harpsichord. I should try in vain to express in words what I feel when I whistle the hymn "In all my earthly doings" really well on a quiet evening and think the words to it.

There are in our thoughts certain trade winds which at certain times blow constantly, and — we may steer and shift however we wish — they are always blown into the same direction. On such November days

*as the present ones, all my thoughts drift between
melancholy and self-disparagement unless some special
current drives me sideways, and often I would no
longer be able to find myself if the two compasses,
Friendship and Wine, did not direct me and give me
courage to fight* against a sea of troubles. *Today my
mind was following the thoughts of the great Newton
through the universe, not without being tickled by a
kind of pride: I am, therefore, made of the same substance after all as that great man, because I can understand his thoughts, and my brain has fibers which re-
spond to those thoughts, and what God proclaimed to
posterity through this man is heard by me, while it
glides over the ears of millions, unperceived.*

*The play of imagination with which I follow the
subtlest turn of a description by Wieland* and create
my own world, through which I stroll like a magician,
seeing the kernels of some slight frivolity blossom into
vast fields of intellectual pleasure — this imagination is,
in its most rapid flight, often attracted by a delicately
curved nose, by an uncovered healthy arm, so force-
fully that nothing remains of its previous motion but
a fleeting tremor. And so I hang in the world suspended between philosophy and the cunning of house-
maids, between the most spiritual vistas and the most
sensual feelings and stagger from those into these until
after a short struggle my twofold Self will come to
rest some future time, and I shall, totally divided, rot
here and evaporate into a pure life there. We two, I
and my body, have never before been* two *so much as
now; sometimes we don't even recognize another; then
we run against each other in such a way that both of
us don't know where we are.*

---

* German poet of the eighteenth century, noted for his subtle, sensuous
imagination.

*How did you like it at this party? Answer: Just
fine, almost as well as in my room by myself.*

Many things hurt me which only annoy other people.

*He can, before you say the Lord's Prayer, enum-
erate ten circumstances to be considered. Thoughts
come to him as if a goblin were supplying them.*

*He kept on hand a little piece of paper on which
he usually wrote whatever he regarded as a special
demonstration of God's grace, and which could not
be possibly explained in any other way. When praying
most ardently he sometimes said:* Dear God, something
to put on my little piece of paper!

*I cannot deny it:When I saw for the first time that
people in my country began to know the meaning of the
radical sign in mathematics, clear tears of joy came into
my eyes.*

P.m. used to say I have surely been saved for some
great crime, since I must overcome so many insults to my
feelings that I have become indifferent to almost everything. If life didn't make a slight difference, it would be
the same to me whether I were elevated at Tyburn **
or at St. James.*

Noticed blindness *on April 9th, 1775.*

*On the evening of April 15th, the Saturday before
Easter, I went for a walk in Hyde Park after tea; it
may have been a quarter of seven. The moon had just*

---

* *P.m.* in Lichtenberg's diaries also means himself.
** At Lichtenberg's time, place of public execution in London. St.
James: the king's palace there.

*risen; it was full moon and it was shining from above
Westminster Abbey. The solemnity of the eve of such
a day made me indulge in my favorite meditations with
voluptuous melancholy. I sauntered down Piccadilly and
the Haymarket to Whitehall, partly in order to look
again on the statue of Charles the First against the
bright Western sky, partly to give myself up in the
moonlight to meditations in view of the Banqueting
Hall, the house through the window of which Charles
the First walked out onto the scaffold. It so happened
that I saw there one of the men who hire organs from
the organ-makers and play while walking through the
streets, until someone calls them and for sixpence has
them play through their pieces. Suddenly he began to
play the beautiful choral,* In allen meinen Taten,** in
such a melancholy way, so much in harmony with my
mood at that time that a shudder of indescribable awe
came over me. There, in the moonlight, under the open
sky, I was thinking of my friends far away. My sorrows
became endurable and vanished entirely. We had walked
perhaps 200 steps beyond the famous Banqueting Hall.
I called the fellow, led him nearer to the house, and
there I told him to play that magnificent hymn. While
he was playing, I could not refrain from singing the
words quietly to myself:*
"Hast du es denn beschlossen, So will ich unverdrossen
An mein Verhängnis gehn." ** *Before me lay the majestic
building lit by the full moon. It was Easter Eve, the
Mediator's death — here through this window Charles
had stepped down to exchange the temporal crown for
the eternal one. Oh God, what is the greatness of this
world!*

*A girl, 150 books, a few friends, and a view about
four miles in diameter were his world.*

---

* "In all my deeds," one of the best-known German church songs.
** "If Thou has decided so, I shall meet my fate willingly."

Something could have been made of his ideas if an angel had organized them for him.

Once the nerves have become so weak that it is impossible for a man to resolve to undertake steps toward his own recovery, he is lost.

Impressions are still alive in my mind made by causes which vanished a long time ago (my dear mother !!!!!!!).

I saw the grave on my cheeks, April 16th, 1777.

To believe that, in order to be liked by posterity, one has to be hated by one's contemporaries — this I was often on the point of believing with so much conviction that I felt an inclination to assail everything.

A grave illness struck Lichtenberg in 1789. It had its origin in an organic ailment, yet his doctors and later medical experts who have read his notes have agreed that his relentless suffering during and after his illness must have been mainly of a neurotic nature. Diaries which have been published only recently bear this out. When, after one and a half years in bed, he tried to return to a more normal life, his personality had changed. Despite the brief feelings of inner peace and joy over his recovery, mirrored in *Amintor's Morning Prayer,* despite periods of new happiness with his wife and children, gaiety had gone from him. He lived the last decade of his life in an almost continuous state of depression and anxiety. Forty-eight years old, he suffered from the feeling that he was aging rapidly; he felt lonely, but tried to keep strangers away from his home and never left it to visit friends or attend social affairs. Nothing could give him joy any longer but nature — carriage rides in the spring, the singing of the

birds in the stillness of his garden outside the city gate
—and recognition from the men whom he himself admired. The anxieties of the last five or six years of his
life were increased by a secret amorous relationship
which was more an affair of his senses than of his
heart and which caused him more torment and feelings
of guilt than happiness. The brilliance of his mind
faded, but his wisdom became more indulgent. His self-
observation went on as ever; a dozen notes, chosen
from the many intended for his autobiography, allow
us glimpses into his inner life at that time:

*E.g.: He was lying down because of abdominal
cramps; this was his only ailment according to the testimony of the best doctors. But the number of ailments he
believed he had was considerable: 1)* marasmus senilis,
*although he was only 46 years old; 2) incipient dropsy;
3) convulsive asthma; 4) slow fever; 5) jaundice; 6) hy-
drothorax; 7) he was afraid of a stroke; 8) paralysis of
his right side; 9) he believed his big arteries and veins
were sclerotic; 10) he had some growth in his heart;
11) a tumor on his liver; and 12) water in his head. A
person reading this might almost believe the twelfth
was the only fear which had some foundations. 13)
diabetes.*

*During my nervous illness I very frequently found
that what formerly hurt my moral sense, now also affected
my body. When Dieterich* once said "May God kill
me," I felt so sick that I had to forbid him my room for
some time.*

*Few people probably send books into the world
without expecting that everyone will now put down his
pipe or will light one in order to read them. I do not say*

---

* Lichtenberg's publisher, landlord, and life-long friend.

only that I'm not destined for this honor — that would be easy — I also believe it, which is a little more difficult and has to be learned.

The worst thing about this illness is that I can no longer think or feel any thing without, at the same time, feeling mainly myself. I see the entire world as a machine which has the purpose of making me feel my sickness and my suffering in every possible way. A pathological egotist. Pusillanimity is the right word for my illness, but can one get rid of it? He who can overcome it would deserve an honorary column, but who will erect an honorary column for the person who transforms himself from an old woman into a man?

O God! if one could only keep always learning in this world, without being observed. *What a heavenly pleasure the knowledge of the stars afforded me in youth. Thou God of justice! I know no fairer times; they were the happiest of my life. The envy and mockery of other people, who know a little more than I do about this or that point, is unbearable. How blissful my life was in those days! Now that everything I do is observed, and by many a person who's not worth half what I am and who opposes to my original endeavor some remark which he's simply learned by heart, they laugh in my face.*

The night from Easter Sunday, 1792, to Easter Monday, I dreamed that I was going to be burned alive. I was very calm about it, which did not please me at all when I awoke. I had been reasoning very calmly about the length of time it would take. I'm almost afraid everything in me becomes thought, and feeling vanishes.

I used to get angry with a feeling of vigor, but now it is with a feeling of passive timidity.

He had even framed a constitution in order to force himself to act, and appointed real ministers — Temperance, once even Avarice. But they were overthrown again and again.

That I always compare the years of an author whose Life I am reading, with my own — something I did even in my youth — is entirely within human nature.

It was a great mistake in my youthful studies that I made the design for the building too great. The result was that I could not finish the upper story, indeed could not even put on the roof. In the end I found myself forced to be content with a few little rooms in the attic which I finished pretty well, but I could not keep out the rain in bad weather. Many others have the same experience!

Trembling, when we are getting weak, could almost make one believe that our will effects our body in a succession of jerks, and that the continuity in our movements has the same relationship to trembling as has a curved line to a polygon (I understand myself). One can be witty at any age, I believe, only it does not proceed in such a steady flow as when we are young. (One trembles then, too.) If we collect the remarks and take out the intervals, then the reader won't be able to notice the decline of strength.

Frequently I have indulged in all sorts of fantasies, and this at times when people thought I was very busy. I realized how harmful this was with regard to loss of time, but without this fantasy treatment — which I usually underwent with eagerness at the season for taking the waters — I should not have reached my present age, 53 years and 1 1/2 months.

*Formerly when I fished in my mind for thoughts or
ideas I always caught something; now the fish no longer
come so readily. They're starting to petrify on the bottom, and I have to chop them loose. At times I only get
them out in pieces and patch them together.*

He had names for his two slippers.

On February 18, 1799, Lichtenberg made the last
entry in his household-diary and wrote to his brother,
concluding a discussion of Kant's and Fichte's philoso-
phies: *All that the really wise man can do is to guide
everything towards a goal, and yet to take men as they
are. Of this Herr Fichte seems to understand nothing,
and in this respect he is a rash and foolish man. — Forgive me, dear brother, I went further today than I intended. That's what happens when one's heart has a
word to say too. Adieu, Adieu.* These are Lichtenberg's
last words in the last of his 850 letters which are preserved. He died six days later, at the age of fifty-six,
after a short sickness, a disappointed man.

He had not made any great discovery in physics
and had not fulfilled the dream of his life — to write the
German novel in which his own psychological observations and social satire would be presented in Fielding's
manner. Nor had he written the great autobiography.
He had left only short pieces and fragments. Yet an in-
visible community of people feel a kind of smiling respect
or sympathy for each other just for reading and loving
these fragments. They look forward to the time when
Lichtenberg will be known more widely as one of the
most deeply original thinkers and most graceful humorists
in the history of Western thought.

APHORISMS

Fourteen of Lichtenberg's sixteen "wastebooks" — variously bound volumes, tightly packed with Lichtenberg's epigrams, *aperçus,* etc., designated by the letters A through F and I through L — are now preserved in the library of Göttingen University. The noted German scholar Albert Leitzmann published most of those entries which are not of a strictly scientific nature; his five-volume critical edition appeared during the years 1902–1908. Two volumes (G and H) have been lost, and most of K has been destroyed, but we know a small part of their contents from editions which Lichtenberg's brother and sons published after the author's death.

Of the over 4,000 entries in Leitzmann's edition — many are merely quotations — we have selected a few hundred; of the others about fifty. All are arranged chronologically; we considered arranging them topically, but Lichtenberg's own order gives the reader some idea of the constant flux of his ideas and the variety of his interests.

Since this READER is not intended primarily for scholars, we have omitted almost all items dealing with contemporary political events, philosophy, literature, and the problems and methods of the natural sciences. A number of aphorisms are included because they show Lichtenberg's skill in coining striking phrases and his delight in them.

Although Lichtenberg wrote on the spur of the moment, his manuscripts contain many cuts and changes, designed to make his style more expressive and particularly more concise. In his *feuilletons,* polemical writings, and commentaries on Hogarth, he often quoted ideas and turns of phrase from his own "wastebooks" — or "thoughtbooks," as he sometimes called them.

It is hard to state how we arrived at the ideas we now hold. No one, or very few persons, can state when they first heard the name of Leibniz. It would be still harder to state when we first arrived at the idea that all men must die; we do not acquire it as quickly as people generally believe. Hard as it is to state the origin of phenomena which transpire within us, how will it be when we want to make such a statement with reference to things exterior to us?

*

The greatest things in the world are brought about by other things to which we pay no attention — petty causes which we overlook and which finally accumulate.

*

The asses perhaps owe the sad situation in which they now live in the world only to the witticism of a wag. It is his fault that they have become, and will remain forever, the despised animal, for many donkey-drivers treat their wards so terribly because they are asses, not because they are lazy and slow.

*

Many conclusions about men's characters could perhaps be drawn from their dreams, if they would report them exactly. But quite a few would be needed, not just one.

*

We would certainly get to know people of peculiar temperaments if the great regions which are now ocean were inhabited; and if perhaps, after some thousands of years, our present *terra firma* becomes ocean and our oceans turn to land, completely new manners and morals will arise, which now would greatly amaze us.

*

43

Violent ambition and suspicion I have always seen going hand in hand.

*

We often strive to subdue some vicious emotion, and try at the same time to preserve all of our good ones. This comes from our method of describing man: we fail to see his character as a very neatly constructed totality, which can be rearranged only by changing the relative position of its various parts. Rather, we regard his emotions as adhesive beauty-patches, which we may shift or throw away at will. Many such errors derive from the languages indispensable in describing the emotions. Thus we always think of the most ordinary meaning the moment we neglect, to the slightest degree, the particular association. Therefore, if a general system of characterization is to be invented, a proper language must first be found.

*

Sometimes, when I had drunk a great deal of coffee and was accordingly startled by everything that happened, I could observe with great precision that I started up in fright *before* I heard the crash. It follows that we hear with other instruments, as it were, than our ears.

*

I should like to know on every evening that second of the past day when my life had the least value, when — if purity of intention and safety of life had a cash value — I would have been worth least.

*

A feeling expressed in words is always like music described in words: the expressions are not sufficiently homogeneous with the thing itself.

*

Really to appreciate a seemingly unimportant piece of good fortune, we must always imagine that it was lost and that we got it back this very minute. But some experience of all sorts of sorrows is needed to carry out these experiments successfully.

*

The critics instruct us to stay close to nature, and authors read this advice; but they always think it safer to stay close to authors who have stayed close to nature.

*

If we could express ourselves as completely as we feel, talkers would find few refractory listeners; and lovers, few cruel ladies. Our whole body wishes, when a beloved girl is about to depart, that she would stay; no organ can convey this as clearly as the mouth, but how is it to convey its message in such a way that the wishes of the other organs are also perceived to some extent? Indeed, it is very hard to give advice about this if one is not yet actually in this situation, and still harder if one has never been in it.

*

There is a certain sort of people who easily make friends with everyone, just as quickly hate him, and then love him again. If one thinks of the human race as a whole, in which each part fits in its place, such people are "fillers," to be inserted anywhere. One seldom finds men of genius among people of this sort, though they are very easily taken for geniuses.

*

Everyone admits that the dirty stories we make up ourselves have a far less dangerous effect on us than other people's do.

*

We are ourselves the measure of the miraculous; if we should find a universal measure, the miraculous element would disappear, and all things would be of equal size.

*

Our nature is so widely constituted that both past suffering and past joys are pleasing in remembrance. Since, moreover, we can more easily anticipate a future pleasure than a future sorrow, we see that painful and pleasant sensations are not even equally balanced in the world; the balance is actually weighted on the pleasurable side.

*

Man's happiness consists of a proper relationship of his traits of character to his emotions; if one trait grows stronger, all the others suffer, and countless combinations result. What we call a "great mind" may just as well be a monstrosity, as a gambler is; but it is a useful monstrosity.

*

The man who lives calmly and cheerfully is the true human being. Such a man will rarely make very great progress in any field, for a machine which has many functions can rarely perform each of them as usefully as one designed only for a single purpose. Therefore, the wisdom of Providence is as much revealed in the rarity of genius, as in the circumstance that not everyone is deaf or blind.

*

All languages have the inescapable defect that they express only the *genera* of concepts and seldom can adequately say what they intend to say. For if we compare our words with things, we discover that the latter are arrayed in quite a different order from the former. The qualities we observe in our souls are connected in such a way that it is not easy to establish a boundary between any two of them, but the words by which we express them are not thus constituted; and two successive, related qualities are expressed by signs which do not reflect this relationship. One ought to be able to decline words philosophically, i.e., to state their relationships under a given aspect by making the appropriate changes. In the geometrical analysis of a line a, one indefinite section of it is called x; the other section is not y, as it would be in ordinary life, but $a - x$. This is the reason that mathematical language has such great advantages over ordinary speech.

*

There is no doubt that creatures may exist whose organs are so delicate that they are unable to reach through a ray of light, just as we are unable to reach through a stone because our hands would be destroyed first.

*

Perhaps a thought is the cause of all motion in the world, and the philosophers who have taught that the world is an animal may have hit upon the notion in this way: they may have failed only to express themselves as exactly as they ought perhaps to have done. Our whole world is only the effect upon matter of one of God's thoughts.

*

Not to exist means to natural scientists — at least to those of a certain type — the same as not to be perceived.

*

Why is it that we are able at times resolutely to ban-

ish a secret sorrow — since the idea that we are protected
by a most benevolent Providence affects us so strongly
— and yet we almost succumb, within the next half hour,
to this same sorrow? That's the way things are with me,
at least. But I couldn't say that I regard my sorrow from
a different point of view the second time, or see it in a
different context — by no means. If this were what took
place, I would not even have jotted down this observation. Rather, I believe that the moral sensitivity of man
is different at various times, stronger in the morning than
in the evening.

*

To become wiser means to become increasingly acquainted with the errors to which this instrument with
which we perceive and judge can be subject. Today the
thing to be recommended to each and every one is caution
in making judgments. If we could obtain only one indis-
putable truth every ten years from each philosophically
inclined author, our harvest would still be rich enough.

*

A landscape can easily be composed of a number of
haphazard strokes, but not a piece of music of haphazard
sounds.

1768-1771

When he was expected to use his mind, he felt like
a right-handed person who has to do something with
his left.

*

The ordinary man is ruined by the flesh lusting
against the spirit; the scholar by the spirit lusting too
much against the flesh.

*

Everyone should study at least enough philosophy and *belles lettres* to make his sexual experience more delectable.

*

I have observed that persons whose faces are somewhat asymmetrical often possess the subtlest minds.

*

Every man has his moral backside too, which he doesn't expose unnecessarily but keeps covered as long as possible by the trousers of decorum.

*

At the comedy, whenever something seemed ridiculous to him, he looked around for someone to laugh with him. When I noticed this, I never came to his aid but looked steadily away.

*

He had outgrown his library as one outgrows a vest. Generally speaking, libraries can become too tight or too loose for the soul.

*

What I mean by "moral ether" is really that spiritual element present in all our actions, even the smallest, and flowing through all of them; it is to be found in "and he took a pinch of snuff" as much as in Corneille's "Qu'il mourût" or his tight-packed "Soyons amis, Cinna."

*

The urge to write books, which — like another, equally strong one — sets in at the time when one's beard begins to grow, began rather earlier in my case. My first itch occurred in the sixth year of the German hexameter * and about the fourteenth counting from my birth. This is

* The hexameter, the meter of Klopstock's *Messias*, was the favorite verse form of the German avant-garde around the middle of the eighteenth century.

a rather ticklish time, and parents and teachers must watch their children carefully. Therefore I'll describe what I felt going on within me, and people will be able easily to imagine how a person experiencing these sensations must look: I found the language in our family rather too flat; here and there I missed the adjectives and felt so inflated when I hit upon some, especially the ones which I'd invented myself.

In woman the seat of the *point d'honneur* coincides with the center of gravity; in man it is located rather higher, in the chest, near the diaphragm. Thence, in man, the buoyant fullness in that region when he embarks on splendid deeds, and thence too the flabby emptiness there when he embarks on petty ones.

*

Undeniably, what we call perseverance can lend the appearance of dignity and grandeur to many actions, just as silence in company affords wisdom and apparent intelligence to a stupid person.

*

It was a rash action, but I did it with that warmth without which my life would mean far less to me than it does now. Finally I went to bed, bitterly reproaching myself, with the feeling that I had lost a good bit of moral poundage.

*

·   Her petticoat had very wide red and blue stripes and looked as if it were made of theater curtain. I'd have paid a lot for a front-row-center seat, but the curtain was never raised.

*

Wit and humor, like all corrosives, must be used with care.

*

If an angel were to tell us about his philosophy, I believe many of his statements might well sound like "2 x 2 = 13."

*

Look out, or your slowness will make my patience run down. On my honor, I shan't wind it up again for your sake.

*

Whenever we change, a lot of things get too big or too small for us; useless, in a word. Just as we outgrow a pair of trousers, we outgrow acquaintances, libraries, principles, etc., at times before they're worn out and at times — and this is the worst of all — before we have new ones.

*

He moved as slowly as an hour-hand amidst a crowd of second-hands.

*

It would not be good if suicides could frequently tell their reasons in the language of absolute truth. As it is, every listener reduces them for himself into his own language; in this way he does not just weaken them: he changes them into something entirely different. In order to understand a person completely, one would sometimes have to be that person. Whoever understands what a personal system of thought is, will subscribe to this. To be alone frequently and to think about ourselves and to create our world out of ourselves, may give us great joy; but in this way we work, without noticing it, towards a philosophy according to which suicide is only right and permissible. It is good, therefore, to hook oneself to the world by means of a girl or a friend, in order not to fall off completely.

*

I don't know, the man had indeed that expression

which one could call an inward looking of the eyes of the mind, which is always a mark of the genius.

*

Listening to his remarks makes you feel how much he is oppressed by his climate.

*

A certain friends of mine used to divide his body into three floors — his head, his chest, and his abdomen. He often wished that the tenants of the top floor and those of the bottom would get along with each other better.

*

Now your hand, my dear. . . . Your mouth. . . . So, more next time. So long.

*

To give great pleasure to a beloved person even by our own pleasure is the most charming thing that a sensitive being can imagine. This is why gracious Nature has promised this premium to the person who would take the trouble of making others resembling himself.

*

We must make people feel obliged to us in accordance with what they are, not we.

*

What fresh views would we acquire if we could for once eliminate from our capital of truisms all that is not intrinsic but has accrued through frequent repetition?

1772–1773

The pleasures of imagination are, so to speak, nothing but sketches with which the poor people play who cannot buy the other pleasures.

*

I saw once in Stade such peacefulness combined with a furtive smile — in the face of a fellow who had succeeded in driving his swine into a bathing place which they usually disliked entering — as I have never seen since.

*

I actually noticed on his face that mist which usually rises during our feeling of bliss when we believe ourselves superior to others.

*

Not greatness of the mind but of the wind has made him the man he is.

1773-1775

I knew somebody who thought of the days of the week in the form of particular figures. One of them, Wednesday, he once even drew on the table.

*

He does not have the gallows on his back, but in his eyes.

*

Teach me how to give strength to my salutary intentions; teach me to will with earnestness what I will; teach me steadfastness where the storms of destiny or an uncovered white arm make tremble the structure that it has taken me three years to build. Teach me to talk to the hearts of men so that my words will not be deflected in the refractory medium of their systems of convictions. Add the genius of Horace, and your glory shall resound throughout the ages.

*

Man is that which thinks, not that which says. Two persons who compliment each other would tear out

each other's hair, if each knew what the other thought
of him.

*

In this expression the thought has too much play;
I pointed with the head of a cane where I should
have pointed with the tip of a needle.

*

A king gives orders that under penalty of death
people shall believe a stone to be a diamond.

*

Just as foolish as it must look to a crab when it sees
a man walk forward.

*

This is a promising young man, a genius coming into
bloom — you can hear that now everywhere. Once I
saw ten of them within three months: five were presented
to me, and I to five. I'm sure nothing will become of any
of them. The frost of imitative talk had already weighted
them all down, as far as I could see.

*

The first satire was assuredly written for venge-
ance' sake. To use it in order to better one's neighbor
— against vice and not against the vicious — is already
a thought which has been prettied up, cooled, tamed.

*

A grave is still the best fortification against the
storms of destiny.

*

He pondered things over so meticulously; he always
saw a grain of sand before he saw a house.

*

With voluptuous anxiety.

In all men of real intelligence we find the tendency to express themselves briefly, to say speedily what is to be said.

*

There is a great difference between *still* believing something and believing it *again*. *Still* to believe that the moon affects the plants reveals stupidity and super-stition, but to believe it *again* is a sign of philosophy and reflection.

*

Nothing can contribute more to peace of soul than having no opinion at all.

*

Whoever has two pairs of pants, sell one and buy this book.

*

His watch had been lying in a faint for some hours.

*

If someone writes badly — very well, let him write! To make an ass of oneself is a long way from suicide.

*

The book had the usual effect of good books: it made the simple simpler, the bright brighter, and the other thousands who read it remain as they had been.

*

Don't make a book out of materials which might properly fill up one issue of a weekly paper, and don't make a complicated sentence out of two words. What that great blockhead says in a book would be bearable if he could condense it into three words.

*

Courage, chattering, and the crowd are on our side. What more do we want?

*

What is a "German character"? What? Tobacco-
smoking and honesty, didn't you say? O you simple
dolts! Listen: be good enough to tell me what the
weather is like in America. Shall I tell instead of you?
All right. It lightens, it hails, it's muddy, it's sultry, it's
unbearable, it's snowing, freezing, windy, and the sun
is shining.

*

The heathen Tacitus, whose eye penetrated, with
Jewish subtlety, down to the devil at the bottom of every
action.

*

Truth has to overcome a thousand obstacles to get
on paper undamaged, and back from the paper to the
mind. Liars are its weakest enemies. The star-gazing
writer, who holds forth about all matters and views all
matters as other honest people do when they have had
a drop too much; the super-subtle, affected "judge of
human nature," who sees and wants to see a man's whole
life mirrored in each of his acts; the good, pious man
who believes in every instance because he is respectful,
who examines none of the things he learned before his
fifteenth year and builds up the little bit he has examined
on an unexamined base — these are enemies of truth.

*

Margate. There, as at all seaside resorts, we recover
a little health and lose our hearts instead.

*

They sell everything down to the last shirt — and
beyond.

*

One sip of reason.

*

Our life may be compared to a winter's day: we are born between midnight and 1 A.M., it's 8 o'clock before day dawns, it gets dark again before 4 in the afternoon, and around midnight we die.

*

Such people ought to be made to wear badges marked with the number Zero, so one could recognize them.

*

It's incredible how much our best words have lost. The word *reasonable* has lost almost all its character; people know the meaning but don't feel it any more because of the mass of "reasonable" men who have borne this epithet. *Unreasonable* is stronger in its way. A reasonable child is a slack, pious, no-good tattle-tale; an unreasonable boy is much better.

*

There are people who think that everything one does with a serious face is sensible.

*

In a little town where each face rhymes with every other.

*

For shame! To quarrel over such trifles is to set up batteries to shoot at thrushes; reasonable people scarcely know whether you dealt the blow or received it.

*

The paths are bordered with nevergreen.

*

He writes in such a way that even an angel's mind stops dead.

*

A good expression is worth as much as a good

thought because it is almost impossible to express oneself well without showing an impressive aspect of what is expressed.

*

Now, after we've gotten to know Nature thoroughly, even a child will see that an experiment is nothing more than a compliment we pay her. It is a mere ceremony: we know in advance what her answer will be. We ask Nature for her consent as great lords ask their Provincial Estates.

*

When he saw a gnat fly into the light and struggle with death, he said: "Drink down the bitter cup, poor beast. A professor sees it and is sorry for you."

*

Yes, I too like to admire great men, but only those whose works I do not understand.

*

Because of his obscure sense of his own perfectibility, man still thinks himself far from the goal even when he has reached it; and reason does not sufficiently enlighten him. What he finds easy, he thinks bad, and so he strains from the bad to the good, and from the good to a type of the bad which he thinks better than good.

*

People are not as simple as their writing is. The best thinking which people do is ordinarily instinctive. If they only realized it! But they want everything to be lovely and the style full of dignity. Their presentation is like that of certain simple persons who say "imp" among themselves and "imph" when they're in society.

*

The progress of the good and the purposeful in the world. If, for instance, it is rooted in human nature that ultimately the Christian religion will perish again some day, it will happen whether people oppose this or not. Going against the stream and obstructing it for a little while makes only an infinitely small bend in the line. Only it is too bad that *we* have to be the spectators and not some other generation; no one can blame us for working as hard as we can to shape our times according to our own minds.

I always think that we on this sphere serve a purpose whose fulfillment a conspiracy of the whole human race cannot prevent. In just the same way a good book will go down to posterity even if all the critical judges should combine to cast suspicion on it — not by satire but with the mien of the innocent lamb and the accent of the lover of truth — even if they should keep absolute silence about it. If it contains a dozen new truths, stated well and vigorously, if the expert in human nature appears in the rest of the work, then a legion of witty magazine writers will be as little able to block its course to eternity as I could fan back the storm or the rising flood with a playing card. *A* man can condemn a good book through envy, lack of judgment, or foolishness, but Man cannot.

*

The secret of the ridiculous is probably Möser's* *bigness without strength*. Strength without bigness is never laughable, but bigness without strength almost always.

*

Man is never more serious than when he is exasperated or praises himself.

*

We should not separate too much, not abstract too much: the great *raffineurs* have made the fewest dis-

* Justus Möser: contemporary historian and critic.

coveries, I believe. The usefulness of the human machine is precisely that it shows totals.

*

If I know the genealogy of Lady Learning correctly, Ignorance is her older sister. Is it really such a shame to take the elder, even though the younger stands ready to do one's bidding? I have heard from everyone who has known the elder sister that she has charms of her own, that she is a good, fat girl who serves splendidly as a wife, precisely because she sleeps more hours than she is awake.

*

The enthusiasts whom I have known all had the dreadful fault that, at the least spark which fell upon them, they always went up in flames like fireworks prepared long in advance — always in the same manner and always with the same uproar — whereas the feeling of a reasonable man is always proportionate to the impression. The frivolous man keeps cold-bloodedly on arguing after his first impression, while the reasonable man turns around now and then to see what instinct has to say.

*

Some people say: Sterne must have had a good heart, otherwise he could not have written like that. Doesn't that seem very simple-minded to you? In the city where Sterne spent most of his time, with Sterne's slyness, faint-heartedness, observing mind, his penchant for tranquillity, with his parties — under such circumstances one can easily reach the point of speaking as if one were sheer feeling without feeling anything.

*

We acquire professors, promising young people; we

acquire books, read, excerpt, and argue ourselves white, yellow, consumptive — and frigid and impotent.

*

People who have read a great deal seldom make great discoveries. I don't say this as an excuse for laziness, for inventing presupposes a far-reaching, original observation of things: one must see rather than be a listener. Association.

*

I don't use the word *devil,* which frequently occurs in my little work, in the sense in which the common people take it, but like recent philosophers, in order to keep peace with all sects. Thus it is rather to be compared with the x, y, z of the algebraists, an unknown quantity.

*

Nothing pleases Apollo better than the slaughtering of a frivolous, irresponsible reviewer on his altar.

*

What sort of an effect must it have on a people not to learn any foreign languages? Presumably an effect rather similar to that which a complete withdrawal from all society has on an individual.

*

Educating the mothers means training the children in the womb.

*

There is no surer way to make oneself a name than by writing about things which have a semblance of importance but which a reasonable man is not likely to take the time to investigate for himself.

*

A on his lips and non-A in his heart.

*

Whoever does not realize this must either have had a poor education or have been hit over the head at some time.

*

In metaphysical proofs of the existence of God it would perhaps be good to avoid the word "infinite" entirely, or at least not to use it until we are clear about the matter itself.

1775–1779

There's no surer criterion of a great writer than that books can be made, *en passant,* out of his incidental remarks. Tacitus and Sterne are models of this, each in his own way.

*

To do just the opposite is also a form of imitation, and the definitions of imitation ought by rights to include both.

*

To read means to borrow; to create out of one's readings is paying off one's debts.

*

It would be worth-while to investigate whether it isn't harmful to devote too much care to bringing up children. We don't yet know man well enough to relieve chance completely of this function. I believe that if our pedagogues succeed in their intention — I mean, if they bring it about that the children are shaped completely by their influence — there won't be a single really great man produced from now on.

*

As soon as a man begins to see everything in everything, he generally expresses himself obscurely — begins to speak with the tongue of angels.

*

To make astute people believe that one is what one is not, is harder in most cases than actually to become what one wants to appear.

*

We, the tail of the world, don't know what the head is planning.

*

I have known people who drank secretly and have been besotted publicly.

*

It rained so hard that all the pigs got clean and all the people dirty.

*

In courteous towns it is impossible to acquire any knowledge of the world; everyone is so courteously honest, so courteously rude, so courteously deceitful that a man can seldom get angry enough to write a satire. These people always deserve compassion. In a word, everything lacks strength.

*

It cannot be denied that some of our modern *beaux esprits* have all the innate talent to become great writers which they could receive from nature; the reason that they are not great writers is that they have not learned anything. They have no surplus and therefore are not able to throw away any gold coins.

The writer who can't at times throw away a thought about which another would have written dissertations, unworried whether or not the reader will find it, will never become a great writer.

*

A book is a mirror: when a monkey looks in, no apostle can look out.

*

Where people know man only from books and see in all matters only what they already know.

*

Lessing's confession, that he had read almost too much for the health of his mind, shows how healthy his mind was.

*

I have already observed elsewhere that everything in the world is diffused into everything and everything is to be found in everything. I mean that everything which we observe and designate with a particular word was already there before it reached the degree which we could observe. The example of the storm: all clouds are one, and can be distinguished only in degree.

*

From the easy order of nature to the forced regularity of a blockhead in his Sunday best.

*

Why is it that disagreeable thoughts pain us much more keenly in the morning, when we awaken, than some time later, when we know that everyone is awake; or when we have risen; or in the middle of the day; or also when we are lying in bed in the evening? I have had abundant experience of this: I have gone to bed quite reassured about certain matters about which I was again greatly troubled around 4 in the morning, so that I often lay awake and tossed for several hours. By 9 o'clock, or even earlier, indifference or hope had returned.

*

In our times, when insects collect insects and butterflies prattle of butterflies.

*

In the theory of parallel lines, people all too often
believe that their conviction is the fruit of explanation
and demonstration — if the explanation of that axiom
can be called a demonstration.

*

The reason that people can retain so little of what
they read is that they think so little themselves. When
a person knows how to repeat sensibly what others have
said, he has usually thought a great deal himself — unless
his mind is a mere pedometer.

*

Merchants, who often hear quite contrary styles
praised every day by people whom they respect for other
reasons, develop so mixed a taste that finally everything
pleases them. Therefore they are right in saying "This
was chosen by such-and-such," rather than saying "That
is beautiful, and that not."

*

To think highly of a matter, people must not see it
complete; rather, a part must be kept hidden for con-
jecture. Thus in most cases we have a lower opinion of
a man after his tenth book than before his first, not because he has written himself out, but because by then
we have enough points known to draw his whole life-
line. Everywhere a well-displayed supply is more pleasing than extravagance.

*

At the end of a complicated syllogism one can con-
sult common sense in about the way that the mathematician makes sure, by a geometrical construction or even a

rougher estimate, that he has not made a mistake. If the
estimate contradicts the calculation, he calculates again
to see in which of the two the error lies.

*

The itch of a great prince, it is said, gave us long
sleeves. In just the same way, the lack of new ideas,
from which a certain formerly popular writer suffers, now
gives us his pompous, puffed-up style, for the inexperi-
enced dunce thinks there must be God-knows-what hidden underneath.

*

The roads keep getting wider and finer the closer
one comes to this hell (London).

*

He has been so long at giving birth without anything coming of it that even now presumably nothing will
come of it unless there's a Caesarean operation.

*

Perhaps a dog, shortly before it falls asleep, or a
drunken elephant has ideas which would not be un-
worthy of a Master of Philosophy. But these are of no
use to them.

*

They had sent a little octavo volume to Göttingen
and got back a quarto in body and soul.

*

He was a busy writer and a very diligent reader of
his own articles in the learned periodicals.

*

What effect it would have on me if I once had to
sit in black clothing in a great room hung all in black,
where even the ceiling was covered with black cloth,

and with black carpets, black chairs, black sofa and only a few wax candles, and was waited on by servants dressed in black!

*

What they call "heart" is located far lower than the fourth vest button.

*

That was way back when time still had no beard.

*

If a later generation were to reconstruct the man of today from our sentimental writings, they would believe he had been a heart with testicles.

*

I believe that the source of most human misery is indolence and softness. The nation which has the most energy is also always the freest and happiest. Indolence never avenges a wrong but puts up with the worst insults and the worst oppression.

*

The metaphor is far more intelligent than its author, and this is the case with many things. Everything has its depths. He who has eyes sees something in everything.

*

The Greeks possessed a knowledge of mankind which we apparently can hardly attain without going through the invigorating hibernation of a new barbarism.

*

To live in fratrimony.

*

Why are young widows in mourning so beautiful?

*

In an ordinance one could decree the sacrifice of verse firstlings.

*

How close may our thoughts come at times to grazing on a great discovery?

*

Just as one says someone "holds an office," while actually the office holds him.

*

Doubt must be nothing more than vigilance, otherwise it can become dangerous.

*

I am convinced that a person doesn't only love himself in others; he also hates himself in others.

*

Man becomes a sophist and super-subtle in fields where he has no adequate store of solid information.

*

Materialism is the asymptote of psychology.

*

An alert thinker will often find more that is instructive and delightful in the playful writings of great men than in their serious works. The formal, conventional, ceremonial is usually omitted from them; it is amazing how much wretched conventional stuff still appears in our way of narrating in print. Most writers put on airs, just like many people when they are having their portraits painted.

*

About the peculiar charm of white paper, bound into a book. Paper which hasn't yet lost its virginity and still shines in the color of innocence is always better than after it has been used.

*

The publisher has had him hanged in effigy before his work.

*

I cannot say that I was his enemy, but neither was I his friend; I have never dreamed of him.

*

It is difficult to feel the monkey-ishness in the human foot, but sometimes I can; then one discovers easily what is human and conventional.

*

An intelligent child who is brought up with a mad child can go mad. Man is so perfectible and corruptible that he can become a madman through sheer intellect.

*

If it is true, as I once read, that no one dies before he has done at least one sensible thing, then M—— has begotten an immortal son.

*

Among the tributes people brought him, he always found the honest name of "enemy" the most pleasing.

*

We keep saying "soul" as we keep saying "taler" long after the minting of talers has ceased.

*

The girl is quite all right; one only has to put another frame around her.

*

We must not believe, when we make a few discoveries in this field or that, that this process will just keep going on forever. The high-jumper jumps higher than the plowboy, and one high-jumper better than another, but the height which no human can jump over is very small. Just as people find water whenever they dig, man everywhere finds the incomprehensible, sooner or later.

*

There is a sort of transcendental ventriloquy through which men can be made to believe that something which was said on earth came from heaven.

*

A philosophical dream book could be written. People have made the *interpretations of dreams* bear the brunt of their precocious zeal, which actually should have been turned only against *dream books*. That's the way it usually is. I know from undeniable experience that dreams lead to self-knowledge.

*

And what is sickliness (not sickness) other than an inner distortion?

*

Just as there are mechanics of genius who do splendid work with a few inferior instruments, there are also people who know how to use their slight learning and to extend their experiences so widely that a so-called scholar can hardly rival them.

*

I commend dreams again; we live and feel as much dreaming as waking and are the one as much as the other. It is one of the superiorities of man that he dreams *and knows it*. We have hardly made the right use of this yet. Dream is a life which, combined with the rest of us, makes up what we call human life. Dreams gradually merge into our waking; we cannot say where man's waking state begins.

*

People always say "How originally the man writes!" To me his style seems by no means unusual; it is the manner of all the fellows who want to say more than they know, and pleases the crowd precisely because it makes them think they understand things of which they don't know a word.

*

Not only is the rainbow different which each of us sees, but each of us sees a different object and a different sentence.

*

I believe that it is far better to draw something from our own selves than from Plato. Him we can misunderstand; we are always close enough to ourselves to make everything difficult easy and to clear up everything obscure.

*

All the shallow great writers of our time.

*

Where affectation begins to be one's true nature.

*

One of the main conveniences of marriage is to be able to pass a visitor whom one can't stand along to one's wife.

*

Dressing young misses like ladies draws all their vanity to the surface (and must do so). Children must and shall have their own costume.

*

God creates the animals; man creates himself.

*

I understand all too well that there are people whose imagination and sentimental enthusiasm leave them not one minute to do something nasty on purpose. However, they do their share all the more abundantly, not on purpose, but with "good intentions" guided by—I don't like to say this—weakness of intellect.

*

For the time being, one must not make the world believe that what we seek can really be found or, worse, has been found. Especially if one has some authority.

*

To discover trivial mistakes has always been characteristic of intellects little if at all above the mediocre. Those who are noticeably superior keep silent or make only criticisms which pertain to the whole. Great minds simply create, without fault-finding.

*

People don't like to choose lot #1 in a lottery. "Choose it," Reason cries loudly. "It has as good a chance of winning the 12,000 talers as any other." "In Heaven's name don't choose it," a *je ne sais quoi* whispers. "There's no example of such little numbers being listed before great winnings." And actually no one takes it.

*

The sounds of the nations are innumerable, and the Englishman has his *th* in all his deeds. One can't imitate his deeds any more than his speech.

*

In a machine as complicated as this world, we are all, I think, gambling in a lottery as far as the essentials are concerned, even though we may have a slight part in determining events.

*

Taking off one's hat is an abridgement of one's body, a making smaller.

*

A thousand see the nonsensicalness of a statement, without finding it possible (or being able) to disprove it formally.

*

A healthy appetite and the high regard for women which is usually combined with it.

*

New glimpses through the old holes.

*

Sickly people often have mastered skills which a decently built fellow would lack either the ability or sufficient resolution to learn.

*

Flabbiheartedness.

*

A man construes all the vague sarcasms he hears as references to himself and thinks people had him secretly in mind.

*

The most successful and therefore the most dangerous seducers are the "deluded deluders."

*

A great strength of feeling, of which so many boast, is all too often the result of a decay of the intellectual powers. I am not very hard-hearted, but the compassion I often feel in my dreams is incomparably greater than when my brain is awake; the former is a pleasure which closely approaches pain.

*

Oh, I know all too well the people who, because of humbled pride or blind ardor, always nest a mile above or below the truth.

*

An Amen-face.

*

Whenever the sophisticated men of the world say "God knows why," it is always a sure indication that, in addition to God, they know an important man who also knows.

*

What do all these conclusions based on experience help? I do not deny that at times they are correct. But are they not equally often wrong? And is that not what I wanted to say? A game of chance.

*

We love ourselves in others. Where we discover goodness, it's the face that pleases us.

*

Some famous works are nothing but the most ordinary sophomoric philosophizing seasoned with unchecked quotations from general travel accounts — all presented with such a ringing of bells and tinkling of cymbals that even critical minds are misled into thinking a festival is being celebrated.

*

Our sensibility is certainly *not* the measure of the beauty of the vast plan of nature.

*

An ass had the task of carrying the statue of Isis, and when the populace honored the statue by falling down before it, he thought the honor had been paid to him.

*

People who have taken no intellectual food for ten years, except a few tiny crumbs from the journals, are found even among professors; they aren't rare at all.

*

This is a very fertile truth: if kept in a sound brain it has, like the coins in Fortunatus' purse, a new one lying beside it every morning.

*

I can't deny that my distrust of the taste of our time has perhaps risen in me to a reprehensible height. To see every day how people get the name "genius" just as the wood-lice in the cellar the name "millipede" — not because they have that many feet, but because most people don't want to count to 14 — this has had the result that I don't believe anyone any more without checking.

*

The astuteness of a man may be measured by the degree of his deliberation about the future or the end. *Respice finem.*

*

How odd it would be if a man's mouth should some day begin to tell his most secret affairs without his being able to stop it; and during all this, he would have to keep complete command of his intelligence.

*

Not at all is really a phrase suitable only for angels; *very little* is more for men.

*

It is well known that the man belongs to the class of the so-called pompous writers who find "lovely" only everything gorgeously fake. Thus the author of the *Letter* says that Versailles compared to Sans Souci had seemed to him like the dwelling of a dwarf contrasted to that of a giant. Now not one word of that is true, nor did it really seem like that to him; but it seemed to him at home that it *had* seemed that way; or it seemed to him that it would be lovely *if* it did seem like that; or, finally, it seemed to him it would be lovely just to *say* it had seemed so to him.

*

Actually there were only two persons in the world whom he loved warmly: one was, at any given moment, his grossest flatterer, and the other was himself.

*

He loved pepper and zig-zag lines.

*

What makes a prolific author is often not his great knowledge but rather that fortunate relation between his abilities and his taste, by virtue of which the latter always approves what the former have produced.

*

I would often rather read what a famous author has cut from one of his works than what he has let stand.

*

His inkwell was a veritable temple of Janus; when it was corked up, there was peace in all the world.

*

Some actions are called malicious because they're done by ugly people.

*

God, Who winds our sundials.

*

First there is a time when we believe everything without reasons. Then, for a short time, we believe discriminatingly. Then we believe nothing at all. And then we believe everything again and, indeed, cite reasons why we believe everything.

*

They feel with their heads and think with their hearts.

*

Books we want to have young people read should not be recommended to them but praised in their presence. Afterwards they will find them themselves.

*

The impulse to propagate our race has propagated a lot of other things too.

*

By reading so much we have contracted a sort of learned barbarism.

*

Indisputably, masculine beauty has not yet been portrayed enough by those hands which alone could do so — feminine hands.

*

One has to get very close to certain persons to perceive the charm which their good, helpful disposition gives them. For just this reason, can't this disposition be completely indiscernible in certain others?

*

At the ball, when the company went out to supper, it had settled around a couple of girls like filings around a magnet.

*

On that day we went to see an English equestrian who had already given his last performance twice and was now getting ready to give his first *very* last performance.

*

While we don't burn witches any more, we do burn every letter which contains a blunt truth.

*

A physical experiment which makes a bang is always worth more than a quiet one. Therefore a man cannot strongly enough ask of Heaven: if It wants to let him discover something, may it be something that makes a bang. It will resound into eternity.

*

As soon as people know that someone is blind, they think they can tell it from behind.

*

A writer must go out into the world, not so much to observe many situations as to get involved in many himself.

*

We are reliably informed that a single so-called racy expression often costs him two to three hours. Such trouble Nature takes to keep men of such years from childish tricks, and such trouble weak minds take to work against Nature!

*

Often, when an acquaintance passes by, I leave the window — not so much to save him the trouble of bowing, as rather to save myself the embarrassment of seeing that he doesn't bow.

*

Seeing ourselves in dreams comes from seeing ourselves in the mirror at times without thinking that it *is* in the mirror. But in dreams the image is more vivid and conscious thinking is slighter.

*

There actually is a sort of reserved and sensitive people who look, when they are happy, like others when they weep.

*

All inventions come through chance, the one closer to the end, the other farther from it. Opportunity and occasion are the inventor; ambition is the improver; confidence in one's powers is power — in the married state and in the learned world.

*

To be sure, he rather lacked polish, but was actually a real zebra among the donkeys, or among his fellows.

*

And thinks that everyone with no trousers on is a Scotchman.

*

Beauty no longer exists in a body from which one has removed the skin; but to the eye of a higher being it would certainly still be there.

*

Where major issues are concerned, I have carefully refrained from anything which my opponents might call inspirations of wit. For anyone who has such inspirations finds it easy, if he sticks rather firmly to his intention, to avoid the consequences of being witty; while usually those who reproach him for it would not themselves have refrained unless forced to by incurable impotence.

*

I can quite easily imagine how easily praise in the newspapers can seduce a man into believing that he finally is what these people claim for him.

*

To me, it's a very unpleasant feeling when someone feels pity for me, in the usual sense of the word. Similarly, when people are really angry at someone, they use the expression, "One has to pity a person like that." This sort of pity is a giving of alms, and alms presuppose need on the one side and abundance on the other, however insignificant it may be. But there is a much less selfish sort of pity which is genuinely concerned, which moves quickly to act and to save, and is seldom accompanied by sentimental melancholizing (*sit venia verbo*).* One could call the former "alms-giving pity" and the latter "pity as an offensive and defensive alliance."

*

Just as one thinks every full holiday is Sunday, and the following day Monday.

*

The scribble-book method is most warmly to be recommended. To leave no idiom, no expression unwritten. We can acquire riches by saving up the penny truths, too.

*

At times we admire the energy of the languages of uncultivated peoples. Ours is no less energetic; our most everyday expressions are often very poetic. Yet the poetic aspect of an expression vanishes when it becomes common-place; the *sound* then produces the concept, and the *image,* which previously was the medium, disappears and with it all the associated ideas.

1779–1788

One man begets the thought, the second baptizes it, the third sires children on it, the fourth visits it on its deathbed, and the fifth buries it.

*

Nowadays beautiful women are counted among the talents of their husbands.

*

* "May I be forgiven for this expression."

Doubt everything at least once, even the statement, "two times two makes four."

*

It is delightful to hear a foreign woman speak our language and to hear lovely lips make mistakes. This is not the case with men.

*

Both the honest man and the scoundrel simply confuse *mine* and *thine*. The honest man regards the former as if it were the latter; the scoundrel does the opposite.

*

There is surely something genuine in religious hatred, therefore presumably something useful. I do wish that this element could be discovered. Our philosophers speak of religious hatred as something which could perhaps be argued away; but surely this is not the case.

*

The intelligent freethinkers are a light flying column, always in the van, always reconnoitering the territory which the solemn corps of the orthodox, with its serried ranks, will also reach after all.

*

A girl, 150 books, a few friends, and a view about four miles in diameter were his world.

*

Often, at night, I've had to laugh at an idea which seemed to me poor or even wicked by day.

*

We don't devour each other; we merely slaughter each other.

*

Oh, how often I have confessed during the night in the hope that she would absolve me, and she has not absolved me!

*

Never undertake anything unless you have the heart to ask Heaven's blessing on your undertaking!

*

I and *me*. *I* feel *me* — that makes two objects. Our false philosophy is embodied in the language as a whole: one might say that we can't reason without reasoning wrong. People don't bear in mind that speaking, no matter about what, is a philosophy. Everyone who speaks is a folk-philosopher, and our academic philosophy consists of qualifications of the popular brand. All our philosophy is an improving of linguistic usage; that is, an improving of a philosophy — of the most common of all, in fact. But the ordinary philosophy has the advantage of possessing declensions and conjugations. Thus we always teach true philosophy in the language of the false one. Defining words is no help; for by using explanations, I don't change the pronouns and their declensions.

*

How many ideas hover dispersed in my head of which many a pair, if they should come together, could bring about the greatest of discoveries! But they lie as far apart as Goslar sulphur from East India saltpeter, and both from the dust in the charcoal piles on the Eichsfeld — which three together would make gunpowder. How long the ingredients of gunpowder existed before gunpowder did! There is no natural *aqua regia*. If, when thinking, we yield too freely to the natural combinations of the forms of understanding and of reason, then our concepts often *stick* so much to others that they can't unite with those to which they really belong. If only there were something in that realm like a solution in chemistry, where the individual parts float about, lightly suspended, and thus can follow any current. But since this isn't possible, we must deliberately bring things into contact with each other. We must *experiment* with ideas.

*

The words *divine service* should be reassigned and no longer used for attending church, but only for good deeds.

*

As long as we don't really describe our lives, recording all our weaknesses, from those springing from ambition to the lowest vice, we shall never learn to love each other. [But if we attempt it,] complete equality, I hope, will be the result. The more it goes against the grain, the more truthful one must be toward oneself.

*

A man who has once stolen his hundred thousand dollars can live honestly ever after.

*

He received very warm — rather burned — thanks.

*

He swallowed a lot of wisdom, but it seemed as if all of it had gone down the wrong way.

*

In the world we live in, one fool makes many fools, but one sage only a few sages.

*

A donkey appears to me like a horse translated into Dutch.

*

He was running a little business in obscurantism.

*

It would be a good idea if some child would write a book for an old man, now that everyone is writing for children.

*

Everyone is a genius at least once a year. The real geniuses simply have their bright ideas closer together.

*

Now people are trying to spread wisdom everywhere; who knows whether, in a few hundred years, there won't be universities to restore ancient ignorance.

*

My hypochondria is really a proficiency in sucking out of every incident of life, whatever it may be, the greatest possible quantity of poison for my own use.

*

He who is in love with himself has at least this advantage — he won't encounter many rivals in his love.

*

How happily many people would live if they concerned themselves as little about others' affairs as about their own.

*

Some people display a talent for pretending to be silly, even before they become intelligent. Girls have this talent very often.

*

Man loves company even if only that of a small burning candle.

*

There is something in every person's character that cannot be broken — the bony structure of his character.

Wanting to change it is the same as teaching a sheep to retrieve.

*

Nothing is judged more carelessly than people's characters, and yet there is nothing about which we should be more cautious. Nowhere do we wait less patiently for the sum total which actually *is* the character. I have always found that the so-called bad people gain when we get to know them more closely, and the good ones lose.

*

Isn't it strange? We always consider that those who praise us are competent critics, but as soon as they blame us, we declare them incapable of judging creations of the intellect.

*

He can't hold his ink; and when he feels a desire to befoul someone, he usually befouls himself most.

1789

"Age (the number of years) makes one astute" — that's true, but this doesn't mean any more than "experience makes one astute." On the other hand, "Astuteness makes one *old*" (that is, remorse, ambition, *chagrin* make the cheeks sink in, the hair turn gray or fall out) is no less true. These daily lessons driven home by chastisement, not on the backside but on more dangerous parts, are a veritable poison.

*

The weakest of all men is the voluptuary — he who lusts after the body or the spirit. I mean the whoremonger or the god-hopper: the one who whores with girls, or the other who whores with religion.

*

The very fact that so many writers go out of their way to point out Frederick the Great's human weaknesses shows more clearly than all the praise of his panegyrists that they regard him as something superhuman. It's not so much that they try to humble him with their fault-finding as that they try to put him on a par with what we call a merely great man.

*

The highest point to which a weak but experienced mind can rise is skill in detecting the weaknesses of better men.

*

"Alas!" he cried when the accident occurred, "if I'd only done something pleasantly wicked this morning, I'd at least know why I'm suffering now!"

*

Why has God made doubleness so pleasurable? Man and woman: the *Two* deserves our attention. Is it perhaps the same thing with body and soul?

*

First the book must be threshed out.

*

Even though walking on two legs isn't natural for man, it's certainly an invention which does him credit.

*

The myths of the physicists.

*

Overwiseness is one of the most contemptible kinds of unwiseness.

*

And now the artificial ruins were gradually becoming natural ones. Ruins to the second power.

*

How did people ever arrive at the notion of freedom? It *was* a great thought.

*

Our theologians are trying by force to make the Bible into a book without common sense.

*

Some say that men have existed who, in writing down an idea, hit upon its best expression at once. I take this with a grain of salt.

*

I believe that nervous diseases can serve to uncover all sorts of relationships. I could burn, cut, prick myself, etc. — all that didn't have any effect on me. But the slightest emotion carried me away. Vain efforts of people to do something, for instance, when somebody couldn't make a horse come to a halt. Music was disgusting to me too, yet I could very well put up with my own janglings, and even with splitting wood on the table with a chopping-knife.

*

The room was quite empty except for a bit of second-hand sunshine which lay on the floor.

*

This is only the faint echo of a severe thunderclap of superstition (of conscience, etc.).

*

This whole theory is good for nothing except disputing about.

*

Non cogitant, ergo non sunt.

*

Sense is order; and order is, in the last analysis, harmony with our own nature. When we speak reasonably, we speak only from our essence and our nature. In order to incorporate something in our memory, therefore, we always try to supply sense or another sort of ordering. Therefore *genera* and *species* among plants and animals, as well as other similarities, including rhyme. In just that category, our hypotheses also belong; we must have some, because otherwise we could not remember things. This has been said very long ago, but one comes back to it again from all directions.

Thus we try to bring sense into the physical world. But the question is whether we can really make sense of everything. Certainly, by much testing and reflection, a meaning can be brought into something which is not sensible for us, or not sensible at all. Thus one sees in the sand faces, landscapes, etc., which certainly are not the intention of these patterns. Symmetry belongs here too; silhouette in the blot of ink, etc. Also the scale in the range of creatures — all that is *not in the things but in us*. Generally one forgets too easily that when we observe nature, we always observe only ourselves, especially our orderings.

*

The fly that doesn't want to be swatted is most secure when it lights on the fly swatter.

*

Sufficient material to hold one's tongue about.

*

His beatings showed a sort of sex drive: he beat only his wife.

*

A fish which had drowned in the air.

*

Just as the supporters of Herr Kant always reproach their opponents for not understanding him, it seems that some others believe that Herr Kant is right *because* they understand him.

*

I made the journey to knowledge like dogs who go for walks with their masters, a hundred times forward and backward over the same territory; and when I arrived I was tired.

*

Health is infectious.

*

A man can really never know whether he isn't sitting in a madhouse.

*

After a Thirty Years' War with himself, a compromise peace was made; but the time had been lost.

*

I am always grieved when a man of real talent dies, for the world needs such men more than Heaven does.

*

There is no more malicious and spiteful creature under the sun than a whore when she finds herself forced by old age to become a bigot.

*

The movement of the seasons is a clockwork in which a cuckoo calls when it's spring.

*

He could split a thought which everyone considered simple into seven others, as a prism splits sunlight; and each one of them always surpassed the one before. And then, another time he could collect a number of thoughts and produce the whiteness of sunlight, where others saw nothing but motley confusion.

*

I've thought for a long time that Philosophy will yet devour herself. Metaphysics has already partially devoured herself.

*

When sitting in a shabby carriage, one can actually put on such airs that the whole carriage looks good, and the horse too.

*

In the last analysis we Christians are nothing more than a sect of Jews.

*

One is lost if one gets too much time to think about oneself, assuming that one doesn't consider oneself as an object of observation, like a specimen, but always as the sum of all that one is at the moment. We become aware of so many sad things that, on perceiving them, all desire to arrange or compare them fades away.

*

It's questionable whether, when we break a murderer on the wheel we aren't lapsing into precisely the mistake of the child who hits the chair he bumps into.

*

One can live in this world on soothsaying, but not on truthsaying.

*

The ponderously learned bear, Dr. Johnson.

*

The priest: You are man-eaters, you New Zealanders. *New Zealander:* And you are God-eaters, you priests.

*

In free France, where people are now free to string up anyone they want to.

*

The world beyond the polished glasses is more important than that beyond the seas and is surpassed perhaps only by the one beyond the grave.

*

The roof-tile may know many things which the chimney does not.

*

With all my easy-going ways, I've always grown in self-knowledge without having the power to improve myself. Indeed, I've often considered myself indemnified for my indolence by the fact that I realized it; and my pleasure in precisely observing one of my weaknesses was often stronger than the annoyance provoked in me by my weakness itself. To me the professor was that much more important than the human being. Heaven guides its saints in strange ways.

*

A golden rule: one must judge men not by their opinions, but by what their opinions have made of them.

*

Condemning people hastily is due mainly to man's instinctive laziness.

*

Instead of saying that the world is mirrored in us, we should rather say that our reason is mirrored in the world. We can do no other than to descry order and wise government in the world, but this follows from the structure of our minds. But it does *not* follow that something which we must necessarily think, is really so, for we have no concept whatever of the true character of the external world. Thus no proof of the existence of God is possible on this basis alone.

*

God's omnipotence in a thunderstorm is admired only when there is none, or afterwards, when it is receding.

*

A worry-meter, *mensura curarum*. My face is one.

*

There are many people who won't listen until their ears are cut off.

*

That's another one of those fellows who believe that man is all finished and the Day of Judgment might as well begin now.

*

Completely to block a given effect requires a force equal to that which caused it. To give it a different direction, a trifle will often suffice.

*

In this town a certain happy dullness of intellect has always been endemic.

*

My body is that part of the world which my thoughts can change. Even *imaginary* illnesses can develop into real ones. In the rest of the world, my hypotheses cannot change the order of things.

*

They sense government pressure as little as they do air pressure.

*

To doubt things which are now believed without any investigation whatsoever, that's the main point everywhere.

*

Everything is good, so to speak, just as a plain strewn with grains of sand contains all possible kinds of patterns; one simply would have to mark the one which is most convenient. However, since one of them is certainly the best, we must create artificial motives. Religion and the philosopher create themselves the best ones. I regard every religion as an artificial system of motives to which authority has given the prestige — partly for subjective, partly for objective reasons — it might otherwise lack. The thing which won't move unless it's pushed must at least be pushed according to the rules.

*

After all, there must be in everything a certain spirit, a view which like a soul directs the whole.

*

Nothing puts a greater obstacle in the way of the progress of knowledge than thinking that one knows what one does not yet know. The enthusiastic inventors of hypotheses usually fall victim to this mistake.

*

God, this great *Qualitas occulta*.

*

Man is a masterpiece of creation, if for no other reason than this: despite all determinism, he believes that he acts as a free agent.

*

Always to search for final causes, not so much for their own sake as to discover how matters are interrelated, and as a purely heuristic device.

*

The word "difficulty" must not even be thought of as existing for a man of true intelligence. Away with it!

*

The more experiences and experiments accumulate in the exploration of nature, the more precarious the theories become. But it is not always good to discard them immediately on this account. For every hypothesis which once was sound was useful for thinking of previous phenomena in the proper inter-relations and for keeping them in context. We ought to set down contradictory experiences separately, until enough have accumulated to make building a new structure worth-while.

*

In your judgment, what is probably the worst, and what the finest deed you have done in your life? A question for one's own privy council.

*

To seek on the grand scale everything that one observes on the small, and *vice versa*. For instance, everything the child says and does, the man will also certainly do in other matters in which he is and remains a child; for, after all, we're only children a few years older. To be sure, we no longer hit the table which we bump against; yet we've invented, for other but similar bumps, the word "fate" and have learned to blame it.

*

To see something new, we must make something new.

*

It's certainly very characteristic of the German to arrange a few experiences in a system as soon as he has them; the Englishman doesn't act this way. Nothing hampers the advance of science more, as Bacon and a hundred others have already said.

*

What a chattering there would be in the world if

people were determined to change the names of things to definitions.

*

Man is a creature who searches for causes; he could be named the cause-searcher within the hierarchy of minds. Other minds perhaps conceive things under other categories, incomprehensible to us.

*

One could call man the "cause-bear" in analogy to the "ant-bear." That's putting it a little strong. The "cause-animal" would be better.

*

Before anything else, extension of the frontiers of learning. Without this, all is in vain.

*

Philosophy is always the art of analysis, look at things as one will. The peasant uses all the theorems of the most abstract philosophy, only enveloped, hidden, tied down, latent, as the physicist and the chemist say. The philosopher gives us the theorems pure.

*

In nature we see not words but always the initial letters of words only, and if we then try to read, we discover that the new so-called words are again only the initials of others.

1793–1799

The immeasurable benefit which language bestows on thought consists, I think, in the fact that words are generally signs for things rather than definitions. What things are — to find that out is the task of philosophy. The word is intended to be, not a definition, but a mere sign for the definition, which in turn is always the variable result of the collective industriousness of scholars.

So be cautious about discarding words which are generally understood, and do not discard them if your only reason is that they might convey a false concept of the thing! In the first place, it is not true that a word conveys a false concept, because I indeed know and presuppose that it serves to distinguish the thing; and second, I don't claim to get to know the essence of the thing from the word.

*

Nomenclature. . . . Here too I consider a carved monarch the best; carved saints accomplish more than those with souls. In changing accepted words, vanity always plays a greater role than utility, for usually the new words become useful only at the point when one takes them for granted as one did the old.

*

Comparison between philosophy and hairdressing: both depend on fashion. Old wigs and old philosophy; the old professors of philosophy creep around, too, like old wig-makers.

*

The French Revolution, through the general idiom which it has brought about, has spread among the people a certain fund of knowledge which won't easily be destroyed. Who knows whether the great won't be compelled to institute barbarism?

*

A: You're twice as fat as before. B: That is the doing of exhausted nature, which no longer has the power to make anything except *fat,* which, if needs be, one can cut away without offending the human condition. Fat,

fat is neither spirit nor body, but only what weary nature leaves behind, valuable to me as to the grass in the churchyard. (Written at twilight)

*

Just let governments of the people take over everywhere: then presumably other conditions will ensue as unpalatable to Reason as the present ones. For that the republican system should be quite free of all harm is a dream, a mere notion. What would it be like if it should become reality? I believe, without wanting to set myself up as a judge, that society will be hurled by revolutions forever and ever from one system to another, and that the duration of each will depend on the virtue of the subjects at the time.

*

The little worry locker, the holy of holies of the innermost economy of the soul, which is opened only at night. Everyone has his own.

*

In the dark ages, very great men often appeared. In those days only a man whom nature had expressly marked for greatness could become great. Now that education is so easy, men are drilled for greatness, just as dogs are trained to retrieve. In this way we've discovered a new sort of genius, those great at being drilled. These are the people who are mainly spoiling the market.

*

Day by day I grow more convinced that my nervous affliction is supported, to a great extent, by my loneliness — if indeed not caused by it. I find almost no amusement any more except with my own mind, which is always kept busy. Since my nerves have never been of the strongest, exhaustion necessarily sets in. I know very well that company cheers me up. I forget myself, or, rather, my brain is receptive rather than active, and so it gets some rest. Thus even reading is a relaxation for me, but not as much as company is, because I keep setting the book aside and again becoming active.

*

A double louis d'or certainly counts more than two singles.

*

Probably no invention came more easily to man than inventing Heaven.

*

Her physical charms were precisely at that exact point where they begin to exchange their power of attraction for that of repulsion.

*

A punch in the stomach doesn't deprive the stomach of all consciousness, but the head itself. In general, people always talk of head and heart and much too little of the stomach, presumably because it's located in the basement; but the ancients knew better. Persius* awarded the stomach an M.A. — and since then it may indeed have increased its learning.

*

When he philosophizes, he usually casts agreeable moonlight over the objects treated. Generally it's pleasing, but it doesn't show one single object distinctly.

*

On K's advice, I got frightfully angry about that matter.

*

Even the gentlest, most modest, and best girls are

* Roman satirist (A.D. 34–62).

always gentler, more modest, and better when they've found in the mirror that they've grown prettier.

*

It is certain, it seems, that we can judge some matter correctly and wisely and yet, as soon as we are required to specify our reasons, can specify only those which any beginner in that sort of fencing can refute. Often the wisest and best men know as little how to do this as they know the muscles with which they grip or play the piano. This is very true and deserves to be pursued further.

*

What splendid shape the world would be in if the great lords loved peace like a mistress! They have too little personal reason to fear war.

*

Now reason "stands out" above the realm of the obscure but warm emotions like the Alpine peaks above the clouds. They see the sun more clearly and more distinctly, but they are cold and sterile. Reason brags about its elevation.

*

Where everyone tries to come as early as possible, the great majority must needs come too late.

*

I've again taken to eating all the forbidden dishes and, thank God, feel just as bad as before.

*

How much depends on the way things are presented in this world can be seen from the very fact that coffee drunk out of wine glasses is really miserable stuff, as is meat cut at the table with a pair of scissors. Worst of all, as I once actually saw, is butter spread on a piece of bread with an old though very clean razor.

*

He kept continually polishing himself and finally became dull before he got sharp.

*

Now, in his old age, some mischievous ideas which he had printed seemed to him like the little spots which a beloved robin, while flying around his house, had made on his books, papers, and furniture. Now that the little creature had been taken by a cat, it was forgiven for the spots.

*

It seems to me that the improvements one can confer on states through argumentative reason are merely slight changes. We make new *species,* but *genera* we cannot create; chance must do that. Experiments must therefore be undertaken in natural philosophy; and in great affairs, one must wait for the proper time. (I understand myself. What I've said before belongs here: one should say not "I think," but "It thinks.")

*

Is reason, or rather the intellect, really better off when it arrives at final causes than when it arrives at a command of the heart? After all, it is surely a very open question which of the two ties us more strongly to the world surrounding us, the heart or reason.

*

Is it really so absolutely certain that our reason can know nothing metaphysical? Might man not be able to weave his ideas of God with just as much purpose as the spider weaves his net to catch flies? Or, in other words: might not beings exist who admire us as much for our ideas of God and immortality as we admire the spider and the silk worm?

*

I think one should think less about science of policing than a policing of science. Astronomy goes too far.

*

Just as men incessantly *die* of old age, other things incessantly *improve* through old age. This also applies to our wisdom.

*

To reduce everything in man to simple principles means in the end, it seems, that we assume there *must* be such a principium — and how can this be proved?

From the GÖTTINGEN POCKET ALMANAC

As editor of the *Göttingen Pocket Almanac,* Lichtenberg was bound by contract to write diverse material for the journal every year from 1777 on, in lieu of rent for his apartment in the house of J. C. Dieterich, his publisher and friend. Written often with reluctance and under the pressure of deadlines, many of these articles show only a few traces of the author's philosophical mind, and their wit is sometimes forced. Many others, however, are forerunners of the nineteenth-century *feuilleton;* some are splendid. Naturally, they are full of allusions to contemporary events, situations, and thought.

The four selections presented here seem to us the most interesting to readers not necessarily versed in the history and intellectual climate of eighteenth-century Germany. In our judgment, they also show Lichtenberg at his best. Three of these selections have been shorn of a few remarks irrelevant to today's readers; the *Consolations,* for example, were disburdened of their astronomical material. *Amintor's Morning Prayer,* intensely personal in mood, yet the product of long philosophical and religious meditation, is practically intact.

Amintor's Morning Prayer

What if one day the sun should not return, Amintor often thought when he awoke in a dark night, and he rejoiced when he finally saw day dawn again. The deep stillness of the early morning, the friend of contemplation, combined with the feeling of renewed strength and re-gained health, awaked in him at once so mighty a trust in the order of Nature and in the Spirit Who guides it that he believed himself as safe within the tumult of life as if his destiny were in his own hand. This feeling, he thought at once, which is not forced or feigned and which affords you this indescribable sense of well-being, is certainly the work of just that Spirit and tells you loudly that now at least you are thinking rightly. Also, this inner recognition of order was nothing other than just this order itself, including the one who was observ-ing it; and therefore it was always the source of his loftiest spiritual pleasure.

Oh, I know (he then exclaimed), this my silent prayer of thanks is certainly heard by Thee Who guidest the heavens. All creatures offer Thee this prayer, each with his own feeling and in his own language. Certainly it is offered to Thee by all creatures, in their thousands, but offered with double joy by me, whom Thou gavest the power to know, through this feeling of gratitude and in this feeling of gratitude, that I am what I am meant to be. Oh, do not trouble (he then said to him-self) this heavenly peace within you by incurring guilt today. How would tomorrow's dawn seem to you if the pure mirroring brightness of your being were no longer reflecting it in your inmost soul? It would be better that dawn never appeared again — or at least not for you in your misfortune.

This way of *living in his God,* as he called it — which bigots who believed rather than thought, because they found it more convenient, interpreted as Spinozism — he had made so much his own that it became his *indestructible* reassurance about the future and his insuperable consolation in mortal danger. One day, when he asked himself, after his morning prayer, whence came this joyful surrender to the Power directing the world and this great sense of security whenever he thought of the future (for this feeling was too firm to be merely a poetic transport), he was ravished with joy to discern that he owed it only to the degree of insight into nature which he had achieved. This degree, he maintained, was accessible to any person of even mediocre endowment, who would carry on the study continuously, free of wrangling, of the mania for innovation, and of all speculating. Everyone will readily believe that it must be delightful to be able to say to oneself: "My peace of mind is the work of my own reason; no exegesis gave it to me and no exegesis will take it away from me. Oh, nothing, nothing will be able to take it away from me, except what reason takes away."

He is certain that the contemplation of nature can give us this solace, for within this solace he lives. Whether it would be a consolation for everyone, he left open. Much depended here, he said, on the way this science was studied and applied. This was a matter which (perhaps like Spinoza's system) should be not taught but discovered by oneself, if it was to cause no harm. It was nothing less than that physico-theological contemplation of suns* whose number, according to one

* Centers of planetary systems. Lichtenberg and his contemporaries were deeply moved by Herschel's discoveries.

style of counting, was put at seventy-five millions, if we
consider the host of clearly visible ones only. He called
these sublime contemplations sheer music of the spheres;
initially it overwhelmed his spirit and almost stunned it,
as with a storm of delight, but finally he became accus-
tomed to it. But the element of this experience — undeniably the best — which always lasted was maintained
everywhere, and especially in that spirit within the order
which was capable of these contemplations: it was a joy
in *one's own existence,* imperceptibly merging with the
persistent study of nature, combined with a *happy,* not
an *anxious curiosity* (if that's the right word) to discover *just what all this was and what would become of it.*

He was, to be sure, much afraid that his friends
would hear only the *words* of the doctrine and not the
doctrine itself, but placed the greatest hopes in his own
attempt to explain it when he would speak about it
some day. Now he thought that the pleasure which the
contemplation of Nature affords to the child and the
savage, just as to men of the most varied culture, must
have as its great purpose, among others: *complete tranquillity about the future and joyful surrender to the
Power directing the world,* give it whatever name one
wishes.

He counted it among the most important events of his
life to have discovered, at least for himself, that, just as we
suffer naturally, we also have natural means to bear these
sorrows with a sort of joy. This philosophy, it is true,
does not abolish transitory ill humor or pain, for such a
philosophy — if it were possible — would also abolish all
pleasure. This he often called his *reconciliation with
God,* against Whom reason could perhaps grumble, and
even with hope of forgiveness, had not that thread been
woven into the course of events which can guide us to
that tranquillity without further aid.

Generally many Biblical *expressions* appeared in his speech. In this connection, he said that it was nearly impossible to tell the same history of the human spirit without at times hitting upon the same expressions and that he believed we would understand the Bible better if we studied ourselves more. The shortest way always to live up to its sublime teachings would be to try once to reach its purpose in another, independent way, paying due regard to time and circumstances. It was easier and more sensible for millions of people, he said, to hear from Heaven, *Thou shalt not steal nor bear false witness*, than themselves to seek the place in Heaven where these words really stand written in letters of flame and have been read by many.

Moreover, he thought that it was of no significance to field-glasses and spectacles whether the light really streamed down from the sun, or whether the sun only made a medium vibrate, so that it merely appeared as if light were streaming down.* But this didn't mean at all that field-glasses and especially spectacles were unimportant. When thinking about spectacles, it often occurred to him that, while man did not have the power to shape the world as he would like, he could grind spectacles through which he could make it appear almost as he would. There were more of such reflections, through which he hoped less to direct friends to *his* way of thinking than to give them hints how to find for themselves the one which would be the safest and easiest for them. And actually it is just so: philosophy, if it is to mean more to man than a collection of materials for disputes, can be taught only indirectly.

* The dispute between the followers of the "undulatory" and the "corpuscular" theories of light.

Why Does Germany Still Have No Large Public Seaside Resort?

Where is there a seaside resort in Germany? Here and there perhaps there is a limited opportunity to bathe in the sea in a remote place, without danger and with comfort — that's probably all that's available. Everyone can, of course, provide that for himself without asking anybody. But where are the places which — like Brighthelmstone,* say, or Margate * and others in England — attract even more people in the summer months than our most famous inland baths and spas? I know of none. Isn't that strange? In almost each decade, a new watering-place is founded and prospers, at least for a while. *New baths cure well*. Given the willingness of our fellow-countrymen, not only to listen to recommendations of new baths, but also really to take the cure there, why does no shrewd speculator think of founding a seaside resort?

In addition to their curative powers, what gives such baths so great an advantage over the inland ones is the indescribable charm, especially for the inlander, of a stay on the shore of the ocean in the summer months. The sight of the sea waves, their flash and the crashing of their thunder, compared to which the highly praised Falls of the Rhine is merely a tempest in a wash basin; the great phenomena of ebb and flood tide, which are always absorbing but never tiring to watch; the reflection that the wave which is now making my feet damp is directly linked to the one which washes against Tahiti and China, and helps to form the great highway

* Lichtenberg visited these places in 1775.

of the world; and the thought that these are the waters to which the inhabited crust of our earth owes its shape, now summoned back within these boundaries by Providence — all this, I say, affects the man of feeling with a power to which nothing in nature is comparable, except perhaps the sight of the starry sky on a clear winter night. You have to come and see and hear for yourself. A walk along the seashore on a clear summer morning, where the purest air brings us appetite and invigoration, makes therefore a great contrast to a walk along the stuffy avenues of the inland watering places.

But that is not all, by far. The rest can only be discussed when we have reached agreement about the region where such a resort could be established. The entire coast of the Baltic is unknown to me, and for my part I would not choose it as long as even a suitable hamlet was available on the North Sea, for in the Baltic the indescribably grand drama of ebb and flood is either completely lacking or at best cannot be observed in the majesty with which it appears on the North Sea shore. There the tide gives occasion to a thousand conversations, and where this natural spectacle is not seen in its full grandeur I wouldn't believe that I was at the seashore.

Much depends on the character of the floor of the sea. But even where the bottom is not favorable, it is easy to introduce a contrivance which removes all discomfort; I've seen it at Deal. To make this understandable, I must first familiarize our readers with the way people bathe in the sea in such places. One climbs into a two-wheeled vehicle, a cart, which carries a hut made of boards, equipped on both sides with benches. This hut, which in appearance is not unlike a very roomy shepherd's cart, has two doors, one opening towards the horse and the driver, the other towards the rear. Such a hut holds quite comfortably four to six people who are mutually acquainted. At the rear is fastened a sort of tent, which can be raised and lowered like a hoop skirt. When this vehicle, called a "machine" at the watering places, is standing still on dry land, the hoop skirt is somewhat raised. By the back door is a suspended, but very firmly attached stair, which doesn't quite touch the ground. Above this stair is fastened a free-hanging rope which reaches to the ground and serves to help those who want to plunge under the surface without being able to swim, or who are timid for some other reason.

Well, you get into this hut and undress while the carter is driving to the sea. At the proper place the driver lowers the tent. So when the visitor, undressed, thereupon opens the back door, he finds a very fine, firm linen tent, whose bottom is the sea, into which leads the stairway. Grasping the rope with both hands, he descends. If he wants to plunge under, he holds the line fast and falls on one knee, like the soldiers firing in the first rank, then climbs up again, gets dressed on the trip back, etc. It is for the doctor to decide how long one may indulge in this pleasure (for it is a pleasure of very high rank). The first time, I'd advise, in order to get acquainted before anything else with one's own physical powers, to plunge under the water only once and then to get dressed and never to exceed the proper time; otherwise the pleasant glow which one should feel on climbing out of the water will change into shivering. Since the fair sex is said, in this too, to express at the beginning some shyness towards the untried, excellent go-betweens between the ladies and Thetis exist in these towns, and very soon they get them to the point of becoming go-betweens themselves. In Margate this function is exercised by young middle-class women who occupy themselves with helping the ladies dress and undress, also with renting a sort of loose garment which, though it floats, nevertheless sustains during bathing the secure sense of being clothed, which is always sacred to innocence, in the ocean as in the densest darkness.

Among these women, as among their distant relatives, the midwives, naturally there are always some who make more of an impression than the others and gain general approval because of their modest behavior, cleanliness, decorum, and obligingness. I knew one who was in style then; she frequently took care of three or four carriages at once. And then it was fun to watch from the window how this siren, when she had finished with one group, would go from one cart to another, often a distance of twenty to thirty paces. It was only the head adorned with headdress and ribbons that one saw; it seemed to swim on the surface of the sea like a merry-go-round head made of pasteboard.

[Lichtenberg turns to the question of location and praises the region of Cuxhaven, near Hamburg.]

In addition there is the continuous sailing in and out of the ships of several nations; they are often majestic. They anchor opposite Cuxhaven, and one can board them or at least visit them in small boats and sail around them, always with the purest air and the desire to eat coming upon you. To be sure, these little journeys, free of danger though they are, frequently become little emetic trips, but they are all the healthier for that. I have read of one of the Roman emperors — Augustus himself, if I'm not mistaken — who undertook such emetic journeys in the pure sea air every year.

For the sake of the healthy patients, I shall also note that all sorts of sea fish and shell-fish are always obtained fresh and, just at this season, the herring, well before it reaches the interior. The delicious oysters, fresh-smelling in the hot sun, and the regal turbot! A mighty support for the cart trade.

And then Helgoland! Small private parties, deserting balls and games of faro, undertake a journey to this extraordinary island. The little emetic experiences *en route* are forgotten in the enjoyment of this grandiose view. The person who hasn't seen anything like this before dates a new life from such a view and reads all descriptions of sea journeys with a new understanding. I believe that every man of feeling who has the means to afford this great pleasure, and does not do so, owes himself an accounting. Never have I thought back with such great, almost painful sympathy of my friends left behind in the stuffy cities as I did when I was on Helgoland. I know nothing to add except: come and see and listen.

No one who knows the local conditions of these resorts needs to be seriously worried about sharing the fate of Jonah. The fish who might eat a prophet are as rare as the prophets. To be sure, the fish there have been eaten with great delight from time immemorial, especially by visitors; but I am not aware that any one of them ever returned the compliment.

Consolations For The Unfortunates Born On The 29th Of February

Say what you will, a man who has a birthday only once every four years is never a man like others. In fact a person who has too few birthdays doesn't seem much happier in many respects than that large class of poor devils who have unknown fathers. What is more pleasant for the immortal being within us than to see that other beings of the same sort rejoice in his existence and his life? Even if their joy is not always quite sincere, all right! It's no less pleasant to see that they still find it necessary to act as if they rejoiced. Sincere joy is a sign of love, to be sure, but the insincere nevertheless indicates fear and respect, which in many cases are infinitely more valuable. Now the unfortunate creature who was born on the 29th of February loses at least seventy-five percent of these expressions of joy, in comparison to other people, as can easily be figured out. That is rather hard. Whatever it is that's forfeited — "good wishes" in prose; a Latin ode or a real poem; or ribbons, flowers, cakes, fireworks, torchlight processions, and cannonades — seventy-five percent of them are gone with the wind, anyway.

Yes, the matter can get very serious. Assuming that the unfortunate is the ruler of an empire or of a municipal school, with the right to extort voluntary presents on his birthday, how can he demand a present which is payable on a day which doesn't even exist three years out of four? Aren't the 29ths of February the true Greek Kalends in the years when this month has only 28? Well, if the Greek Kalends are only a poetic Nothing — a pretty phrase created by sublime ancient pedantry — the 29ths of February, three times in four, are a real, solid, prosaic Nothing of ordinary life and daily housekeeping. That's an entirely different matter. Of the former we speak, but this we feel.

So far we have treated only the material side of this deprivation; on the moral side, the loss is much greater still. For since every human being seriously makes up his mind on his birthday to do or give up something (for instance, like Dr. Johnson, to get up earlier in the future or certainly to read all of the Bible next year), our unfortunates naturally are deprived of these salutary resolutions too. And it's clear what will happen to the fulfillment if one can't even get as far as the resolution.

But they still have New Year's Day, someone says. —— That's no answer, for ordinary people have that too. And last and saddest: this disaster, like many another, is getting worse towards the end of this century. For when the year 1796 is past (the last leap year in this century) we won't have another for eight years. Thus a child who was born on February 29, 1796, and died on, say, February 28, 1804, would become eight years old without having experienced a single true birthday, unless one excepts the miserable day on which it was born, which ought not to be counted at all and in the true congratulatory sense of the word is no real birthday.

I wouldn't even have touched upon this ridiculous topic if the question, *When shall a person born on February 29 celebrate his birthday?* had not been raised rather seriously in a famous magazine and left unanswered. Here is the answer and the consolation:

To be sure, a man is born on a certain day, at a certain date; but his entry into the world, his first drawing breath, is the work of a single second. At this point in time, the sun stands at a certain point of its ecliptic.

Therefore a given individual will be exactly one year old the next time the sun stands again in the same point of its ecliptic; and the legal day which contains that instant is the person's birthday in the true sense, whatever the calendar calls it. This, I think, is very clear.

The problem, "When shall I celebrate my birthday if I was born on the 29th of February?" can thus be perfectly solved. Put in the style of a recipe or a set of instructions, it would run somewhat like this:

1) Have someone tell you the second, minute, and hour of your birth, or take the day from the church register. But in the case last-mentioned, since your birth did not last all day, you must assume some definite time: for instance, mid-day.

2) Look up the location of the sun (its longitude) for this instant in an astronomical calendar.

3) Similarly, look up in the calendar for the year in which you intend to celebrate your birthday, the day when the sun will have exactly the same longitude. This day, whatever it is, is your birthday.

If you proceed in this way, you will notice something which will amaze you, assuming you're wholly ignorant of this matter: namely, that if you had been born on any other day — for instance, May 1 — you would nevertheless, under certain conditions, celebrate your birthday on different days, at times on April 30, at times on May 2. Even the birthdays of the most exalted potentates are frequently celebrated incorrectly. Therefore the man born on February 29 isn't always the only one who has to celebrate on different days of the month from the one which the usual method assigns him. This is based on the circumstance that the year does not consist of exactly 365 days but of about 365 days and six hours, while we can't possibly bother with such fractions of days in our ordinary affairs. Thus actually the year is no better off than we or the exalted potentate. At least the hour of its birth is incorrectly celebrated, three times out of four. Often one rejoices jubilantly at the death of the old year when it still has eighteen more hours to languish, and congratulates the new one eighteen hours before it is born.

Well, the upshot is, briefly: If a person wants to celebrate his birthday, or rather just that hour when the *date* and the *time of day* both come out right, every human being in the world can celebrate correctly only once in four years. Therefore the man born on the 29th of February is acting quite rightly if he celebrates now on February 28, now on March 1. The man born on some other day who celebrates it according to the date is often actually mistaken, but no one notices it. So in this case, as in thousands of other happenings of life, it's a matter of situation and circumstances. If they are favorable, a man may be thought wise despite all his errors; if unfavorable, a very lost sheep indeed, despite all his wisdom.

A Dream

It seemed to me as if I were soaring far over the earth, facing an old man whose glorious appearance filled me with something much loftier than mere respect. Each time I raised my eyes towards him, an irresistible feeling of reverence and trust flowed through me, and I was just on the point of casting myself down before him when he spoke to me with a voice of indescribable gentleness. "You love to investigate nature," he said. "Here you shall see something which can be useful to you." Saying this, he handed me a bluish-green ball, with tints of gray here and there, which he held between his index finger and his thumb. It appeared to be about an inch in diameter. "Take this mineral," he went on. "Test it, and tell me what you've found. Right behind you, you'll find all the tools needed for such analyses, in perfect condition. Now I'll leave you, but I'll come back to you at the proper time."

When I turned around, I saw a beautiful hall with all sorts of instruments; it didn't seem as strange in my dream as later when I woke up. I had the sense of having been there frequently, and I found what I needed as easily as if I myself had laid out everything beforehand. I inspected, felt, and smelled the sphere. I shook it and put my ear to it, as if it were a geode.* I raised it to my tongue. I wiped away the dust and a sort of barely noticeable film with a clean towel, warmed it and rubbed it on my sleeve to test it for electricity. I checked it against steel, glass, and the magnet and determined its

* A hollow nodule of stone, lined with crystals or minerals, which produces a noise when shaken.

118

specific gravity, which I found to be between four and five, if I remember correctly. All these tests turned out in a way which showed me that the mineral wasn't particularly valuable; I also remembered that I'd bought marbles of that sort, or at any rate not very different, three for a farthing, at the Frankfurt Fair in my childhood.

Nevertheless I then proceeded to the chemical test and determined the component parts in percentages. Here too the result was not significant. I found some clay, just about the same amount of calcareous earth, but much more silica; finally iron and some cooking salt also appeared, and also an unknown substance — at least, one which, while it had many properties of familiar substances, had others peculiar to it. I was sorry that I did not know the name of my old friend, otherwise I would have given it to this kind of earth, in order to pay him a compliment. Incidentally, I must have proceeded very accurately in my analysis, for when I added up everything I had found, it made exactly 100 per cent.

I had just drawn the last line of my computation when the old man appeared before me. He took my paper and read it with a gentle, hardly noticeable smile. Then he turned towards me with a look of heavenly kindness and seriousness, and asked: "Do you know, mortal, what it was you tested?" The whole tone of dignity with which he spoke now clearly proclaimed the celestial being. "No, Immortal," I cried, casting myself down at his feet, "I do not know." For I no longer wished to refer to my little bit of paper.

The spirit: Then know: it was, on a miniature scale, nothing less than — the whole earth.

I: The earth? Great, eternal God! And the ocean with all that dwell within it — where are they?

He: They hang there in your napkin; you wiped them away.

I: Alas! and the sea of air and all the glory of the dry land?

He: The sea of air? That was probably left over there in the cup of distilled water. And as to your glory of the dry land, how can you ask such questions? That is imperceptible dust; some is clinging here to your coat sleeve.

I: But I didn't find a trace of silver and gold, which rule the globe!

He: Bad enough. I see I must help you. Know then: with your steel you cut away all of Switzerland and Savoy and the finest part of Sicily, and you completely ruined and overturned a whole stretch of Africa, more than a thousand square miles, from the Mediterranean Sea to Table Mountain! And over there, on that pane of glass—oh! they just dropped—lay the Cordilleras; and what flew into your eye before, when you were cutting glass, was Mount Chimborasso.

I understood and kept silent. But I would have given nine-tenths of the life remaining to me to have had again my chemically destroyed earth. But confronted by such a brow, I simply could not ask for another. The wiser and kinder the giver, the more difficult it is for a poor fellow, if he is a man of feeling, to ask for a gift a second time, once it occurs to him that perhaps he did not make the best use of the first. But, I thought, this glorious being with his fatherly face will no doubt forgive me a new request. "O great, immortal being," I exclaimed, "whoever thou art, I know thou canst do it: enlarge a mustard seed to the thickness of the whole earth, and allow me to examine the mountains and strata, till the germ develops."

"How would that help you?" was the reply. "In your own planet you already have a granule magnified, in your eyes, to the thickness of the earth. Make your

test there. Before your transformation, you will not reach
that other side of the curtain which you seek, neither on
this nor on another granule of creation. Here, take this
pouch, test what is in it, and tell me what you have
found." As he left he added, almost in jest: "Understand me aright; test it chemically, my son. This time
I will stay away longer."

How happy I was when I again had something to
examine; for now, I thought, I will be more careful. Look
out, I said to myself, it will gleam, and if it gleams it's
surely the sun or some other fixed star. When I opened
the pouch, I found, quite contrary to my expectation, a
book in a simple binding. It didn't gleam. Its language
and script were not of any known sort; and although the
strokes of several lines seemed rather familiar when
hastily looked at, they were, when more closely examined,
actually just as little known as the most complicated. All
I could read were the words on the title page: "Test this,
my son, but chemically; and tell me what you have found."
I can't deny that I found myself somewhat perplexed in
my vast laboratory. What? I said to myself, I am to investigate the contents of a book chemically? After all,
the contents of a book is its meaning, and in this case
chemical analysis would be the analysis of rags and
printer's ink. When I reflected for a moment, things suddenly became clear in my mind, and with this new light
an irrepressible blush of shame came over me. Oh! I
called, more and more loudly, I understand, I understand! Immortal being, oh forgive, forgive me; I comprehend your kindly reproof, I thank the Eternal that I
can comprehend it. — I was indescribably moved, and
with that feeling I awoke.

LETTERS

Lichtenberg was a very talented letter-writer; like so many other eighteenth-century figures, he must have loved to "correspond." About 900 of his letters are preserved. Most of them are quite long and so admirably adapted to the recipient that they seem frequently to reflect *both* personalities as well as the character of their relationship. In most of his letters, Lichtenberg speaks to his correspondent animatedly and persuasively. In later years, when his depressions set in — and especially after his illness of 1789–90 — he found letter writing difficult, "as hard as jumping over a fence." A mysterious pain in his hand, apparently of psychosomatic origin, served as an excuse for endless delays; Goethe and Kant, among others, had to wait many months for replies.

But even then, his heart and his charm, his tact and his wit went into his letters, and they reflect his intellectual and his erotic alertness. We have selected some which show qualities not so easily discernible in the aphorisms and the essays: his warmth and kindness, as in writing a birthday letter to an old man or fictitious admonishments to a little child; his joy in observing nature and his power of describing it. We have felt free to cut passages which presumably are not of interest to most readers. Major omissions at the beginning and end of the letters are indicated by the conventional four dots.

Life In London

TO CHRISTIAN GOTTLOB HEYNE*

London, the 17th of April, 1770

Noble Sir,

*Most Honorable Herr Hofrat,***

A week ago today, after a very fatiguing journey of fifteen days, I finally arrived in this enormous city, in better health than I had expected. It is incredible what an effect the crowd of new objects, which I have not always been able to fit into my head at once, has had on me. The most recent experience always made me completely forget the previous one, and I am still living, really, in such confusion that I, who formerly could fill sheets of paper with town gossip, am much perplexed about sifting out of my London experiences and the chaotic mass of things I could say enough material to fill a little letter. I have seen the sea, some warships of 74 guns, the King of England in the Houses of Parliament, in all his glory with the crown on his head, Westminster Abbey with the famous graves, St. Paul's, the Lord Mayor moving with great state through a throng of many thousands, all shouting *huzza, God bless him, Wilkes and liberty* — and all this in a week. You, Sir, will easily believe that all this, happening at once, must be to such a retiring soul as mine what a week of university banquets and wedding parties, with no rest nor

* Professor of Eloquence at the University of Göttingen; a famous classicist. (1729–1812)

** Title of honor given to high government officials and eminent university professors.

sleep, would be to my body. Moreover, I live in a house here where I have neither time nor repose to collect my thoughts, and as at a court I must dress twice a day, dine at 4:30 and often at 11:30 at night, usually in a large company.

If one goes out, the distraction on the street is still greater; the tremendous uproar everywhere, the mass of new things wherever one looks, and the throng of chaises and people are the reason that one usually reaches one's destination late or not at all. Recently this happened to me: I went out with the firm resolution to go to see Herr Dieterich's correspondent in the Strand, but before I could get there I got stuck at silver shops, shops with wares from India, with instruments and the like, so that I barely had time to get home in time to dress, and Mr. Elmsley's house was not reached on this expedition. The places I have looked at, I visited in Lord Boston's* chaise and in his company; otherwise I would perhaps still be lodged in an inn between here and St. Paul's. Since I shall probably return to Göttingen with the young Adamses, and earlier than I thought, I'll save up all descriptions of what I've seen until then.

I would much like to stay here, but it would have to be under different circumstances. I have been received here in such a manner and treated with such respect as I could in no way expect; but this means that I had to accustom myself to a style of living which can never be mine in the future, for which it is too late anyway in my case, and which I utterly dislike. If I should actually begin to take pleasure in it, I would be completely lost. But it would be the more pleasant for me if I could live more to myself and more humbly, even if I were to pay for this happiness by performing tasks which I would not

---

* His host. Lichtenberg had tutored one of Lord Boston's sons at Göttingen and was visiting England at his invitation.

take upon myself at home. I already have some very eminent friends here, among whom I can also number Lord Marchmont, who recently spoke with me in public in the Houses of Parliament and next day, quite alone, visited me in my room, but I don't dare to make any such suggestion since I would certainly offend honest old Lord Boston gravely by so doing. . . .

I remain your very humble servant and friend,

G. C. Lichtenberg

English Ladies

TO JOHANN CHRISTIAN DIETERICH*

London, the 19th of April, 1770

Dearest Friend,

I am infinitely obliged to you for being surety for me; you are a friend in need, of whom I have had very few. I hope soon to be back again, for I don't find things as advantageous as I'd thought, despite the fact that I'm really living what a Darmstadt head forester would call a blissful life: I wish that every honest fat man who travels to eat and drink were in my place. In a word, I live (against my will; that's the worst of it) really like a Prince Elector, and I'm convinced that if I lived this way a whole summer, my taste might perhaps be tuned too high and become eternally dissonant with my purse.

British food is simple, they say; that's true, you find few complicated dishes, but they have such a host of simple things that it would be foolish to combine them. In wines they are inexhaustible. First, they eat at midday, and then they drink at midday, two completely different things. At the latter occasion the women are no longer present — this for all sorts of reasons: firstly, so that they don't pilfer the secrets of state from the men; secondly, that no secrets are pilfered from them. At tea they come together again; it doesn't last long and each party keeps its secrets as best it can during this short time. In the evening, or in plain German at night, it's no better — I mean about eating and drinking; about the secrets it is definitely worse.

---

* Book dealer in Göttingen; Lichtenberg's publisher, landlord, and life-long friend. (1722–1800)

In London everything is for sale which you can't get for any money in other countries, and some you get quite free — all jumbled together at all hours of the day in all the streets, prepared in every manner, clothed, bound, framed, wrapped, unbound, rouged, preserved, raw, perfumed, in silk and in wool, with or without sugar. In a word, what man can't get here for money, he shouldn't look for in this real world.

Ordinarily I don't like to write about women and I almost never do, unless the woman I write about, or the man I write to, is something extraordinary. Now I'm in a situation where both conditions hold, and so for once I'll really write myself out about women. As soon as one sets foot in England (I assume, however, that one has something besides feet) the extraordinary beauty of the women at once strikes the eyes of the student as well as the philosopher and the book dealer; and the number of these beauties increases continually, the closer one gets to London. For the man who is not really sure of himself in this respect, I know only one way out: let him at once go back with the next packet-boat to Holland. There he will be safe. In my life I have known very many beautiful women, but since I've been in England I have seen more than in all the rest of my life together, and yet I've been in England only 10 days. Their extraordinarily pretty dress, which could give some appeal to a Göttingen fruit-woman, raises them still higher.

The house-maid who makes a fire in my fireplace every day and warms my bed (with a warming-pan, of course, friend) comes into the room at times with a black silk hat, at times with a white one and with a sort of train, carries her warming-pan with as much grace as some German ladies their parasols, and kneels before the bed in this costume with such nonchalance that you would think she had 40 such trains; and at that, speaks an English which is hardly to be found in your best English books, my friend. If your heart can stand quite a bit, come over; I'll guarantee you'll be chattering English before your bed has been warmed 40 times. All the streets teem with such creatures. The prettiest are the milliners (it was one of them who cost Lord Baltimore 120,000 talers) and another species, of whom I have nothing to say except that there are no examples of their ever costing a man 120,000 talers.

In a single hall, in the House of Lords, I've seen over 200 of the ladies of quality; imagine, 200, each of whom would have been worth at least 150,000 talers to Lord Baltimore. This makes 200 times 150 thousand; that alone would be 30 million talers, just the women as God made them, without including a bit of diamonds and lace and pearls and such in the estimate. That is quite a capital sum! Now I really am tired of writing about the English women, and generally I think that if one can't stay here long, like me, it is better to look than to write. Meanwhile, I beg you not to include this report about English women in the *Gotha Calendar,** not for my sake but for that of the German women. They don't mind if one praises the ladies of Lima as long as one wants to, but the English women are somewhat too close for them. History tells us that the men of Lower Saxony once before marched towards England *en masse.* Very profound political reasons are adduced as the cause, but we don't need them at all: the good Saxons were running away from their wives. So no word of my description must appear in the *Calendar.* . . .

Your most devoted friend and servant,

G. C. Lichtenberg

* Published by Dieterich.

Lonely In Hanover

TO JOHANN CHRISTIAN DIETERICH

Sunday, 29th of December, 1771

My dear Dieterich,

. . . You can't imagine how well I have been accommodated here; I have a room with carpets and a bed so big and soft that one can hardly jump into it without thinking evil thoughts. And today I passed by the kitchen and wanted quite innocently to look at the fireplace. Suddenly my eyes bumped into another pair so hard that I really feel it still; truly, I would rather have bumped the tenderest part of my elbow six times against the stove. But so help me, *here* I want to look at absolutely nothing but stars; only it just occurs to me that the Devil with his satanic dazzlings can often give other people's eyes such an appearance that one would swear they *were* stars. . . .

G. C. Lichtenberg
présentement à Hanover.

Tuesday evening, March 17th, 1772
at 9:30

Dear Dieterich,

. . . This is the fourth day I must sit at home on account of my eyes. Meanwhile, I am not without most pleasant company: Privy Secretary Schernhagen spends the whole afternoon with me from time to time. Tomorrow I'm going out, whatever comes of it. I have been advised to take quicksilver cures; but it sounds so *malho-nette*, a quicksilver cure — rather die gallantly than use quicksilver. There's no question: the slight change of air, food, and way of living, or whatever it is, has caused a noticeable change in me. If I drink a single glass of wine in the evening, I am sleepless half the night; several times I've got up again; and if I drank a bottle, I would be sitting in the police station a few hours later, just as sure as I'm sitting in my room now — the devil is so strong within me then. There is something mightier than origi-nal sin at the bottom of this. Between us, I think I have fallen into a hectic fever.

But if, as I greatly wish, it should prove to be that vivifying power which the sun, now rising even higher, instills in the spring into all living creatures from aspar-agus to girls — in brief, into everything which breathes or puts forth roots — fine! If it is this disease, it will be cured without Zimmermann.* Because of my eyes I can't write any more this evening, but I don't want to go to bed yet, so I'll light a pipe and put out the light, to think of my friends with undisturbed clearness for an-other quarter of an hour. Smoking in the dark is really a pleasant occupation, and if one is in good health it comes, I think, right after kissing in the dark; so good night ——

I am your faithful servant,

G. C. Lichtenberg

Hanover, March 21st, 1772
Saturday morning at 8 o'clock

Dear Dieterich,

Good morning, for the first time from my new room,

* J. G. Zimmermann, a famous contemporary physician, noted also as the author of *On Loneliness* and other literary works. (1728–95)

which is twice as large and twice as handsome as my other one.

God, what a peasant girl I just saw! She was wearing a fine napkin on her head, tied under her chin. I still can't understand how I know that she had a napkin around her head, for to the best of my knowledge I kept looking straight into her eyes and at her lips. Unfortunately she had nothing to sell which I needed, and *vice versa:* what I needed was not for sale. Good God, I thought, what are all the eye-salves of mortal apothecaries compared with Thine! — and with this thought I turned my eyes away, so that as little as possible of the salve should fall on my heart. I was on the point of answering your letter, and then the peasant girl came between us; now, since she's gone, let's get down to our work.

Here I don't even have a dog to whom I can say "Du" (I have to put this down so abruptly to relieve my heart somewhat, which just swelled up at a certain thought). I wanted to buy myself a parrot today, but the fellow demanded 6 louis d'or; the creature would gladly have stayed with me. I will very willingly spend one louis d'or a month and hire someone whom I can call "Du," who can be pinched in the cheeks and is made of fine stuff. If I don't soon do something about it, I already sense what things will be like: I'll read in the Bible four times a day, get yellow circles under my eyes, and begin my letters with: "Your Honored favor has been received, if Your Esteemed self is still in good health," etc.

My greetings to all our good friends, and be sure that I'll always be your faithful brother,

G. C. L.

A Provincial Party

TO MRS. DIETERICH

Hanover, the 20th of May, 1772

Dearest Friend,

In order to tell you fully and properly how much your most charming letter pleased me, I'll briefly tell you the story of the day on which I received it. Note well how everything gets increasingly agreeable, and how fate has built over a foundation of annoyance a most elegant structure of agreeableness.

Seven in the morning, at the summer house.

Schneider: * Forgive me, are you already awake, Herr Professor?
The professor: Yes. "Are you already awake?" I've already been awake for three hours. My head aches so atrociously. Did you bring the coffee?
Schneider: No! But the President of the Court sends you his regards and asks for the honor of your coming this afternoon for a cup of soup.
The professor: O hang it! That's what I thought. Everything has to happen at once (*turning his face to the wall again*), but I have no clean stockings.
Schneider: Yes, you do, sir.
The professor: Well, you know what to say, and bring the coffee — quick!
Schneider: Oh, I know what to say — and with that the cheerful fellow disappeared behind the scenes with his usual willingness, which was made doubly swift by the

---

* Lichtenberg's servant.

134

thought that he would have my four dishes to eat alone this afternoon. So much for the servant! But the master, he lay in bed, sleepy but unable to sleep, tormented by headache and still more by the sentence which had been pronounced on him: to have to dine *en gala* this afternoon with a large company.

Half past eight. Magistrate von Münchhausen enters the room. His intention was to tell me that he would pick me up at noon in his chaise, for he too was to dine at the President's. He stayed until around eleven, and during his visit I somewhat forgot that "sentence."

Quarter past eleven. I go into town; the sky clears up; my head does too, somewhat.

Half past eleven. The wig-maker falls upon me with his comb, and I with my knife upon a piece of bread and Limburger cheese, for dinner is not till 2 o'clock. He combs and I chew till a quarter past 12. The day gets very fine, and I almost forget that I am to be taken to the place of judgment in three-quarters of an hour. Today is mail day, I thought, perhaps I'll get an answer. This thought makes it possible for me to rub my hands courageously and get dressed with all the self-denial of a philosopher.

One o'clock. I hear a chaise rattling up, and my heart changes its rhythm and shifts from an andante into a murky.* But it wasn't the right one, and I thank Heaven for this delay.

Ten minutes after one. O Lord, now another one rattles along as if the Devil himself were sitting on the coach-box, and it stops. Today is mail day, I said to myself. Professor, Heaven surely numbers all the beats of an anxious heart just as exactly as the hairs of our head, and if It watches over sparrows, how much more will It

---

*A piece of harpsichord music, having a bass consisting of broken octaves.

watch over a professor who, after all — with the exception of one particular talent, perhaps — is so much better than a whole spit full of sparrows. I thought some
such thing, and climbed into the carriage.

Two o'clock. A large but very pleasant company at
the Herr President's. Five ladies were there; the professor sat between two of them. They must have been of
very noble birth for they didn't have a spark of haughti-
ness, just as everything at the whole table went on very
amicably and agreeably, whereas behind our chairs stood
8 to 9 Presidents of the Chamber, Privy Councillors,
and Field Marshals *en livrée*. The one lady on my right
was very young. She probably made the great discovery
of her vocation in May or June (those are the right
months for it), 1770; thus she was probably 16. She had
so transparent a skin that I almost could have felt her
pulse with my eyes, I believe. Once, just as I was offering
her a plate of crab-tails, I brushed against her arm, down
where it joins the hand, with the outside of my right
hand — I can still show you the place. I wouldn't have
minded that it felt delicate, but it seems to me it was so
utterly fragile. The other, on my left, spoke a great deal
with me, was somewhat older, but encased in an equally
delicate skin. They seemed to be sisters, for they called
each other "Du" at times, over my head, and probably
they hadn't drunk a pledge together.

Four o'clock. Two glasses of English beer, three
glasses of Rhine wine. It's getting finer and finer. The
sun is sinking, and I keep rising. Some cups of coffee,
standing up, and some very jolly talks with the honest
old President.

Five o'clock. Leave-taking. (Not as hard as the one
from Göttingen.) I get into the carriage with Herr von
Münchhausen, and we drive down the lovely avenue to
Herrenhausen. Here we get out and take a much-needed

walk. Better and better! In every hedge a nightingale sat, as the poet says.

Seven o'clock. We fly to town, for the fellow drove like a young Englishman. I am set down at Herr Privy Secretary Schernhagen's, to whom I had been invited the day before. Now (finer and finer) he gives me your letter. I ran through it only hastily to see if it had any unpleasant news. That shall be my dessert, I thought, and sat down at a cheerful table. At eleven-thirty I go to my quarters in town, read your letter a good ten times, and go to my repose, which hadn't been over for a quarter of an hour when I took up my pen to tell you all this. This was the 19th of May, the day, I remember, when people in Darmstadt take the orange trees out of the greenhouses, and when the good season begins. Could I have celebrated it in a better way? . . .

I remain with the most devoted friendship and the most consummate esteem,

Your utterly devoted servant,
G. C. Lichtenberg

Pumpernickel and Girls

TO JOHANN CHRISTIAN DIETERICH

[Osnabrück,* September or October, 1772]

Dear Dieterich,

. . . It's now quite the wrong season to buy a ham; people generally have only one or two left which they won't gladly part with, or for only a high price.†

Pumpernickel, on the other hand, is always to be had, for the Westphalians pray daily: *give us this day our daily pumpernickel.* So you'll certainly get that, along with a pair of Westphalian dancing shoes which I've already bought — you shall do a dance in them for me when I arrive. If I come myself, I may also bring some ham. For you will barely be able to eat pumpernickel, and Christelchen** won't be able to at all; it's almost as if one were eating the grain raw. I have often tried and once had a piece served me which contained about twenty peasant-size bites. I bit some off with a serious air. "Is it possible that you can't eat the bread as God made it, the bread that gives the peasant girls here their fine skin, liveliness, and firm flesh?" I asked myself, and began to grind it between my teeth, for it never is milled. I chewed on; it was horrible. At times all the chewing made me laugh, and I gave the remaining 19½ bites to the horses. At times I indulged in devout contemplations: what a God that must be, Who makes girl's flesh out of this sawdust. At times my fancy became more daring: let's wait until the sawdust has been transubstantiated,

---

* In Westphalia, famous for its ham and pumpernickel.
† I swear that this is seriously meant.
** Dieterich's wife.

138

then it will suit you better — but in any case the horses could count on the 19½ peasant-size bites. I haven't been able to make any more progress so far. The pumpernickel before its transubstantiation into —— is something ghastly, but after transubstantiation, something the like of which no mortal baker has ever baked or will bake. — So much about the pumpernickel and its transubstantiation. . . .

Little Sybil

TO JOHANN CHRISTIAN DIETERICH

Oxenbridge, November 25th, 1772

O Friend,

If you could see how I sit here and write: my two feet put under my little Sybil, next to me another chair on which I'm writing; because of lack of space on the chair the inkwell is also under little Sybil, in my left hand I hold (it just came within a hair's breadth of falling!) a red-hot baked apple and suck at it. My right hand oscillates from the letter to the inkwell and from the inkwell to the letter, and the head (by which I mean me) doesn't worry a country library about what the hand is doing there. In any event I'm sitting warm. If only hard coal like this could be had in Göttingen too. A hard-coal stove is a real companion; and because the little oven keeps me warm, costs money, and I always find something in it to stir and stoke, I have devoted a sort of friendship to the thing and given it the name little Sybil. Now let's see, what *was* it I wanted to say and — now I've forgotten it.

Assure Christelchen that she is in my good graces.

Lichtenberg

"Oxenbridge" — I must remind you of this to save my honor — is not a pun fabricated by me, but this is actually supposed to be the origin of the name of Osnabrück.

The Queen of Denmark

TO MARIE TIETERMANN*

Stade, May 19th, 1773

Noble and Highly esteemed Demoiselle,
. . . In Celle I watched the Queen of Denmark ** dine and stood opposite her almost half an hour. It was the best opportunity to see her. When she dines, everyone is allowed in the hall; at the time I was there, about thirty spectators were present: twenty-six maids and apprentices, two middle-class girls, a professor, and his servant. The Queen is very stout and has a pair of piercing eyes. She ate with a better appetite than I've had in ten years. While she was eating (for which she used her spoon) she let her left arm lie on the table and listened very closely to everything that was said, turning her face with an attentive expression to each person who spoke. A few times she laughed very heartily, but for the rest she was rather quiet, for which the aforesaid healthy appetite may have helped to account. She sat with her hair done carefully and her neck bare; around it she had a very simple necklace, but something must have been wrong with it on this day, for she frequently had to fuss with it. Her dress was of thin blue silk. The company at table consisted of ten people, of whom two were men. On the rampart in Celle she has had two tents put up, where she breakfasts; during the daytime, if the weather permits, she walks through the streets of

---

* Housekeeper at the "Römischer Kaiser" Inn in Osnabrück, where Lichtenberg had stayed in 1772.
**Queen Karoline Mathilde, banned from Denmark, resided in a castle in Celle.

the town and frequently gives her hand to the children to kiss. She is uncommonly loved there and certainly deserves to be. . . .

Your very devoted servant and friend,
G. C. Lichtenberg

A Sea Voyage

Stade, the 19th of July, 1773

Day before yesterday at three o'clock I arrived at Brunswick happy but very tired, half roasted by the sun, with my mouth covered by blisters, clothing daubed with pitch, and a smell like a dried flounder, after a journey of eight days on sweet and salt water. I'd be able to fill a little book if I were to tell and describe for you, honored Sir, all the pleasure, the heart-felt sadness, the views and curious little incidents which occurred on this trip — especially if I should pad a bit some of the least sentimental part with occasional remarks, as they would well deserve. So today I'll select only a few episodes here and there, with the solemn promise to supply all the rest in the future, if not in writing, then certainly by word of mouth.

The company, which had been decreased even on the day of departure by the prophecies and divinations of timid persons, consisted, at the end, of Captain von Hinüber, who had assumed the direction of the whole affair and to whom alone we were indebted for the great comfort, order, and cleanliness on our ship; Lieutenant Zandré di Caraffa, a very courteous and withal most merry fellow, who played a great role during this trip; Lieutenant von Rönne, who had the strongest physique of us all and got seasick first; various other gentlemen; and — Me. Besides us there were the skipper with two sailors, three servants, and a female cook — thus sixteen persons in all. We were equipped with provisions of all sorts;

* One of the friends Lichtenberg made in Hanover in 1772.

among other things, with a big cage full of chickens, and with guns, muskets, fire-crackers, shells, and seven small cannon. For ballast we had taken on twenty large barrels filled with water, and two more with drinking-water. The cabin was divided into three parts by two rows of barrels; we dined in the center, on the right were our bunks, and on the left the servants'. In fine weather we took coffee and tea on deck, facing in all directions, in all attitudes and positions.

From the start the wind was against us, so that we had to tack out to sea. Here it was against us too, but where it had seemed only to tease us before, it now proceeded to real violence; it blew so strongly, straight from Helgoland, that our pilot, whom we'd wisely taken on board earlier in Cuxhaven, said to our skipper: "Listen, Skipper, we aren't getting anywhere, and I'm afraid tonight we'll get a stiff breeze." We were actually at a place where a great many ships come to grief, so we turned right around and sailed before the wind to the Neues Werk,* where we dropped anchor and spent two nights and a day. Staying in this roadstead is particularly interesting, for at low tide we strolled as far as two miles from our ship, shot larks, snipe, caught crabs with our hands, mussels for the kitchen and for collections; and at high tide we sailed about in our longboat. At the end of the second night, a pleasant south wind set in with the ebb tide; in a short time it regained the ground we had lost before. At sea a calm beset us, but the weather was so pleasant that we, who had no interest in making money out of this journey, unanimously consider this day the most agreeable of our whole trip. The sea was all pearl-colored, smooth as a mirror, and towards the west, beneath the sun, it seemed to be burning. The dolphins and seal accompanied our ship and for

* A little island in the mouth of the Elbe River.

this honor were occasionally saluted with a bullet. We got to see all sorts of unusually shaped animals, and everywhere were the little shrimps, swarming like midges in the air and sunning themselves.

It may have been about six in the evening when Helgoland came in sight, and before it vanished in the dusk, it appeared dark blue against the red sky. As soon as it got dark, our south wind visited us again, and we were carried along swiftly to the island, off whose shore we cast anchor between 11 and 12 at night. About two miles before the island a barrel buoy is stationed to warn passers-by of a rock adjacent to it. You will believe without my mentioning it, Sir, that we all turned our attention towards discovering it in the dark, especially since our pilot had told us that same day that quite recently a ship had perished there. Passengers and sailors leaned down over the bow of the ship and looked for it. I *stood* behind them and looked over their heads and had the luck to see it first and called aloud: "There's the buoy!" The helmsman, who saw it himself the next moment, altered his course slightly and we swept past; it was a joy to watch.

What made this night particularly remarkable to me was the phosphorescence of the sea water, which I had never seen before. It was not a matter of single sparks, say, or quickly vanishing faint flashes, but the foam on the waves seemed to glow in its entirety, which, since these waves were numberless, presented a display of fireworks probably as good as the one the artillery will set off at Hanover. To me at least, it was more attractive, much as I love fireworks, and I know your taste so well, Sir, that I am probably safe in maintaining that you would gladly have done without all the splendors of the artillery in return for my fireworks. I had a pail of it hauled up, and when I moved my hand in it the little waves shone in various places, approximately as an obliquely falling light tends to be reflected therein.

The pitcher which follows was filled by me from the fiery source; I'm forwarding it right away since the water in the pitcher could lose some of its quality before fall. It will hardly shine any more, as even the sea does not shine in every wind. I shall be eager to hear what you, Sir, will say about its taste. — Barely had day broken when I crept on deck to see the true shape of the island, of which I'd formed all sorts of images along the lines of the little I had seen the day before. But its true shape surpassed all my imaginings by a very great deal. The whole island consists of a red, very much hardened marl, traversed by white veins. According to people's testimony, it towers 30 to 40 fathoms above the surface of the sea. The top soil on the island is not much more than four feet thick. The number of people is very large for this small place. Everywhere it teems with children, many of whom we saw going quite naked; they swim with a skill I'd never seen before. For three pennies, which I gave a ten-year-old boy, he swam quite a distance out to sea and turned over in the water so that only his feet could be seen; suddenly he turned another somersault, like a dolphin, and came up head-first.

A special kind of weariness, which I feel in this weather, prevents me from going into further detail. You will excuse, Sir, the confused way in which I have here related matters which are perhaps of no consequence. . . .

At the Seashore

TO FRIEDRICH CHRISTIAN LICHTENBERG *

Stade, August 13th, 1773

Dear Brother,

. . . Now something about Stade, where I've been living for twelve weeks and shall perhaps live eight more. The place is smaller than Darmstadt and is inhabited by a rude and superstitious tribe. Most of them seriously believe that I was sent here by the King to make a slight adjustment in the terrestrial globe on account of the many wet years, and that spirits come to me at night, which gives me such a reputation here that I am the talk of the town and all the surrounding country.

The town is about as far from the Elbe as Bessungen is from Darmstadt.** A pleasant path leads there, and if one does not want to walk, one can also get there by water for one penny in a pretty boat. The Elbe is about four miles wide there and constantly full of ships of various nations, sailing to Hamburg or returning from there for the open sea. On the other bank, the fertile coast of Danish Holstein is seen. If I want to, I can go to Hamburg every day for four pennies. Recently I spent four half-days there and must confess that I hadn't thought that there was a place in Germany where one could form so adequate an idea of the grandeur of London and Amsterdam as this city. By the harbor is a building called the Tree House with a gallery on its roof, from which you definitely have one of the loveliest views in Germany, according to the unanimous testimony of all

* Lichtenberg's younger brother, who lived in Darmstadt.
** About eleven miles.

travelers. I think that a sentimental fellow who was brought there blindfolded and then opened his eyes on that roof would fall in convulsions like the man whom Cheselden * operated on and cured of cataract. I cannot possibly launch into a description of this view. I'll only mention that a man can see at one glance hundreds of three-masted ships, any one of which is an astonishing sight by itself. There the light, graceful English ship with its sharp keel — you can see its speed at a glance — lies next to the round, heavy Dutchman, who gladly sails more ponderously in order to load on more cheese; and then comes a ship which returned a few days ago from catching whales, clumsy and heavy as a church, with patched sails, dirty all over. There lie Spaniards and Portugese and Russians, and in the rigging, which looks like a spider web from afar, men climb like spiders. Everything teems with life: repairs are made, there is loading and unloading, and everyone who is awake is hard at work. Suddenly you can see the sails of one of these buildings fill out; and, greeted by joyful shouts of the sailors on the neighboring ships, down the magnificent stream it goes, with a motion whose majesty is unequaled on this earth, to fetch further riches — with many a poor devil on board who today has lived his last happy day. For me, who love trips on the water and everything concerning the sea almost to excess, this is a pleasure which I prefer to all others; it can bring tears to my eyes.

Recently — would you believe it? — I even made an eight-day voyage again, which, after all, cost me only about twenty talers. I went over to the Danish island of Helgoland and, since the waves were very high, and because I always stayed up on deck while the others lay in their bunks, I had the pleasure to be so knocked

---

* William Cheselden, a London doctor. (1688–1752)

about by the motion of the ship that I thought I'd be smashed into bits. This time I didn't get sick, although my servant almost spewed his guts out of his body. On that morning it blew so strongly — though there was no actual storm — that we covered a forty-mile course in four and a half hours. To tell what other trips I took besides the one to this island would lead me too far afield. I brought back six jugs filled with sea water because some persons in Hanover and Göttingen expressed the desire to taste it. Presumably you know that sea water is phosphorescent at night when certain winds blow. On this journey I fully enjoyed this beautiful phenomenon; as our ship made the sea foam, it was as if the sun were shining there on piled-up pieces of tinsel; and when we spat or pissed into the sea, which experiment almost all of us performed without regard for the ladies on board, there always seemed to be a sparkling on the water. On this eight-day journey I was tanned almost black by the sun and the sea air. When I roll back my shirt-sleeves, the color of my hand contrasts so much with my arm that people think I have gloves on or had put my hand into a dilution of glycerine. . . .

I am your faithful brother,
G. C. Lichtenberg

The Voyage Again

TO MARIE TIETERMANN

[Stade, beginning of September, 1773]

Most Nobly Born,
  especially Honored Mademoiselle,
  most valued Friend:

A well-known coward in Osnabrück has dreamed that
I am dead, I hear, and since the dreams of waking cowards
are said to come true far less often than even the dreams
of sleeping ones, I take this as a promise of a long
life. In the meantime I've undertaken all sorts of journeys, including a little sea voyage, and generally I've
been so distraught that I've hardly written to anyone,
and have mainly neglected those who would be the first
to cover such an oversight with the cloak of friendship.
If you, dearest friend, had been a "Most Nobly born
Fräulein *von* Tietermann," I would perhaps have sub-
missively taken the liberty of most humbly laying a few
lines of nonsense at your feet, but since you are something far better, since you are my friend and my little
Marie, I thought: Oh I know, she is so good, she will
certainly forgive me. She can not seriously believe that
I am dead, for in that case I'd have been the least polished
of ghosts if I hadn't appeared to her at least once, tugged
on the sheets, moved a few chairs, knocked over a couple
of spits, or at least rumbled in No. 5 as if Old Nick were
lodging there. No! I am very well here, at least as far
as the weather permits. Indeed, I've frequently been at
parties where I was almost the only one who was not
holding his cheeks.

On a sea voyage to the Danish island of Helgoland and thereabouts, which I, with eight officers, undertook only for pleasure and needed diversion, I was burned almost black by the sun. I did not get seasick, although it blew so hard one time that we covered forty miles in four and a half hours. The whole trip was most pleasant though it only came to twenty talers a person, all included. We had on board three large kegs of wine, an incredible lot of victuals, among which were also a number of live chickens, three servants (among them Heinrich, who is now in very bad shape and almost useless), and a young unmarried woman as cook. As you can easily imagine, the girl must have had courage, since she ventured on the sea, where no authorities are recognized, alone among twelve males, not counting the sailors. Yes, and she was even young and beautiful. But we were the right men for this, all models of virtue; and she had too much pride for the servants, who were either frightened most of the time anyway, or sick. We were on the water eight days and never ate or slept on shore. The seasickness first attacked Miss Cook; then an officer; after that, all three servants; and finally two more officers. But in most cases it was over in a few hours; two of the servants were the worst off.

We sailed out of Cuxhaven with a very bad wind and promised some people there to return if things shouldn't go well. We did work against the wind for six hours, but when the waves began to get too high and we weren't in the best of locations, we turned about, but did not go back to Cuxhaven, in order not to have traveled the whole way in vain, but anchored in a very safe area, where we lay all night and the next day and waited for a better wind. Since we had not returned to Cuxhaven and had not been sighted by the ships which did arrive there, people began to think that we must have gotten onto the Kälbertanz (a very dangerous spot, where ships are lost every year) and been wrecked. Yes, it was even printed in the paper that a ship with *distinguished* passengers on board had been lost. This caused a great fright here, for each officer had his charmer, and one probably had several in Stade; they all believed it was all up with us. My charmer in Stade does not read the paper or perhaps she too would have been frightened. In Göttingen the news arrived that I had drowned along with eight officers of Bock's regiment.

And we, we were so gay! When the weather was fine (and most of the time, at least, it was) we were out early to enjoy the most splendid spectacle on earth — I mean the rising sun on the open sea; then some of us went back to our cabins again. Towards seven we were all on deck, where we breakfasted; some were conversing at one end of the ship, some at another, others were making observations; the servants, meanwhile, were serving tea, coffee, and toast. Between nine and ten we drank a delicious cordial (it agrees with one very well on the water) — all this among the most friendly conversations, all sorts of quips, and everything that keeps one cheerful. At one o'clock we ate, and better, I must confess, than I eat here in Stade; everything was prepared with English cleanliness, and the drinking at table was pretty heavy at times. Between four and five we drank coffee on deck again, and at eight we again had an equally fine meal. After dinner we smoked on deck and watched the phosphorescence of the sea, spoke of the stars, and told all sorts of stories. Time never hung heavy on our hands, for a ship newly descried or some marine animal gave a new impulse to conversations; at times, too, we fired the cannon or shot at sea birds. Doesn't that sound like fun? It's fine when one has a good conscience and no debts and is not in love — I mean hopelessly in love.

None of these burdens weighed me down, nor ever shall as long as I retain the use of my five senses; one sleeps better, sails better, and in the end makes his way to Heaven better. Don't you think so, Marie dear?

Your

most devoted servant and true friend,

G. C. Lichtenberg

On the Power of Love

TO FRIEDERIKE BALDINGER*

Wednesday, 8 in the morning, February 19th, 1777

I can't continue the way I had begun yesterday, nor do I want to. So I'll lay a smaller foundation for a smaller building, for you to — blow down. Yet, to judge from a mysterious premonition, this letter won't turn out very short either; it will certainly turn out unusual. I'm risking a lot if I ever meant much to you, for I'm risking the loss of everything. You shall read not only my thoughts on *falling in love* and the power of *woman* here in one epitome, but I want also to give you a brief sketch of my method of philosophizing, not merely to persuade you more easily about the first point, but that you may also more easily forgive me. I shall say everything in the most straightforward terms which occur to me, and must therefore ask for two things. First, that you imagine that I'm writing neither to *man nor woman,* but to a *soul* capable of reason. Then, since this concept might not be as familiar to many a person as it is to you, send back this letter, as soon as you've read it, again under seal. Only now I realize that one of these requests concerns your mind, the second your heart. Therefore I must add yet a third: that granting these requests should not depend on the attention which heart and mind will be able to pay to this *confusion,* for it might be that they would be utterly disappointed.

The question, "Is the power of love irresistible?" or, in other words, "Can the charm of one person affect us

* Wife of Lichtenberg's colleague, Professor Ernst Gottfried Baldinger.

so strongly that inevitably we must fall into a state of misery, from which only the exclusive possession of that person can extricate us?" I've heard answered with a "yes" countless times by young and old. Often they raise their eyes to Heaven and fold their hands over their hearts, signs of deepest conviction and of nature's unconditional surrender. I too could answer with a "yes"; nothing would be easier or cheaper, and in the future I'll do so again, to be polite. Possibly I'll do so seriously, if future experiences enrich the privy council from which I'm now philosophizing; but I doubt it very much, because a few examples, which will battle on my side once they are properly elucidated, suffice to refute the whole thesis forever. As I say, I've heard and read the thesis upheld countless times, in prose and verse. But how many among its upholders have seriously examined it? At least I'm not aware that any one has done so, and perhaps no one really has; for who is likely to examine a matter to whose truth the cuckoo and the nightingale, the turtle dove and the gryphon, bear witness with one voice — at least, if one may believe the sweet and the bitter bards of all ages. At their philosophy, however, the philosopher fortunately laughs just as much as the sensible girl laughs at their love. I have, I believe, adequately explored this question.

I maintain with utter conviction: love's irresistible power to make us either supremely happy or supremely unhappy through one object is the poetic twaddle of young persons whose mind hasn't attained full growth, who don't yet have a voice in the council of mankind in determining what is true, and who are mostly so constituted that they won't ever be able to have one. Here I declare again, although it's obvious, that I don't mean the procreative urge; that *can* become irresistible, I believe, but surely nature did not imprint it on us to make us supremely unhappy or supremely happy. To believe the former makes God a tyrant, the latter makes man an animal. And yet all the confusion in this dispute stems from not sufficiently distinguishing this urge, which appears in very different forms, from rapturously sentimental love. People defend love and attack love, and one party understands one thing and the other something else. That's all for this morning.

Thursday, 9 o'clock

Good-hearted maidens have taken the expressions *Heaven on earth* and *bliss,* with which many poets have labeled happy love, as eternal, unchangeable truth; and maidenish youths have believed it after them, though it's only the insipid chatter of young star-gazers who did not know what was heaven or what was earth. These appellations are true only to the extent that it's true that maidens are goddesses. The Greeks, who were not only the wisest and bravest but also the most voluptuous people on earth, certainly did not think that girls were goddesses or that association with them was paradise or that their love was irresistible. They didn't even show them that respect for the weaker sex which one would have expected from a free people, not to speak of a tender-hearted one. They used them to breed those masses of organized flesh out of which they later formed heroes, sages, and poets — and for the rest, let them go their own way. Women dwelt in the inmost part of the house and did not attend social gatherings with men. In this way, to be sure, they lost all opportunity to educate themselves up to the level of such clever persons, and so they had to become continually worse and more contemptible. That genuinely great men did pay court to some of them — this distinction they had first to earn through particularly outstanding intellectual talents, and these visits were not of the sort paid by men "in love." The Greeks did not reckon as a merit women's ability, bestowed by nature, to satisfy an urgent appetite in a pleasant and useful way. I think they were very much in the right, for it's a transaction in which both parties gain. The expressions *give away one's heart* or *one's favors,* again, are poetic flowers of speech. No girl gives her heart as a gift. She sells it either for money or for honor; or she exchanges it for another, an arrangement in which she has the better of it or at least thinks she has.

But why do I cite the Greeks to you? Does not a very sensible people exist today, free from the cult of enthusiastic love, which is both ridiculous and indolent; a people to whom alone we owe progress in useful studies, the improvement of man, and all great deeds? Do you know which people I mean? Certainly, you're well acquainted with it. It is the community of active, reasonable, *vigorous* spirits which one finds spread over the whole earth, though many a town may have none of them: the healthy, useful, happy rustic whom our simple-minded poets celebrate and admire (as they do nature, as a matter of fact) without knowing him, and whose happiness they desire without being willing to choose the way which leads to it. My blood boils when I hear our bards envying the happiness of the peasant. You want to be happy as he is, I'd always like to say, and at the same time stay the fop you are; that won't do at all. Work the way he does; if your limbs are too delicate for the plow, work in the depths of science; read Euler * or Haller ** instead of Goethe, and bracing Plutarch instead of *Siegwart.**** Finally, learn to enjoy your rustic girl like your rustic fare — transfigured and sea-

---

* Leonhard Euler, famous Swiss mathematician. (1707–1783)

** Albrecht von Haller, Swiss scientist and poet, important in the history of physiology, botany, anatomy. (1708–1777)

*** A sentimental novel by J. M. Miller, published in 1776, written in emulation of *The Sorrows of Young Werther,* the work by Goethe most widely known at that time.

soned by hunger — as your peasant does. Then you'll
be happy, as he is.

Not nobility of soul nor sensitivity, but idleness
(or at least work which leaves the mind idle) and ignorance of the great attractions of science, in which
there is absolutely nothing about *love and wine,* are the
sources of that dangerous passion, which never — I'll
venture this as a general statement — has .gained power
over a truly manly soul. If love makes a person seek out
the wilderness and chat with the moon in all seriousness,
he certainly has a screw a little loose somewhere, for
one weakness seldom occurs alone.

I have very lofty ideas of the greatness and dignity
of man. To follow an urge without which the world
could not endure; to love the person who has chosen
me as her only companion, especially since, according
to our customs, this person clings firmly to my heart by a
thousand other things, and influences me in the varied
relationships of adviser, friend, business associate, bed-
comrade, plaything, jolly brother (sister doesn't sound
right) — that surely I consider no weakness but clearly
plain duty; also, I don't think it's within our power
not to love such a creature. But that a girl should be
able by her charms to steal a man's peace, so that he
would have no taste for any other pleasure, and that it
should not lie within his power to resist this inclination
— not in the power of a man who can bear poverty,
hunger, scorn of his own merit, go to his death for honor's
sake? — that I'll never believe. It may be true for the
fop, the soft weakling who has never tried to resist in
any matter, or the voluptuary who knows no higher
pleasure of the mind than the consciousness that a pretty
girl loves him, but certainly not for a man of real soul.
If such a man ever made a statement of that sort, it was
a compliment to the ladies, indeed a very impolite one,

because it's a lampoon against all reasonable men; and yet it's a question if it is a compliment to the ladies at all. Many men think the female sex so weak, vain, credulous, and conceited that they believe everything they're told if it concerns the power of their charms. But these men, if one can call them that, are very greatly in error. Don't you agree, madam?

But if we capriciously indulge in a notion based on such an urge, and not only don't try to resist it but are even proud of not resisting, and think ourselves initiates into the mysteries of all-delighting nature as soon as we can build such love-castles in the air — O, God, what wouldn't be called irresistible in this world!

The love which I think proper for a reasonable man is related to the kind against which I write, as the just tear shed by the true man at his mother's death is to the ill-bred howling and tearing of hair of the weak-souled mob. And I know well, even if I preached till Judgment Day, the number of those who steadfastly resist those consequences of love will always be the smaller. But why should that be more surprising than that the people who bear their misfortunes with courage and calm are likewise very few? We must not base our conclusions of what man might be someday on what he is in Europe today. On other continents he is indeed different, far different. . . .

The Death of Dorothea Stechard*

TO A. L. F. MEISTER**

[Göttingen, the middle of August, 1782]
My dear Colleague,

What do you say about our household? Two hours after my excellent girl had been carried away, the little Dieterich girl died. Every hour they asked about each other's health, and their graves are close to each other. The little Stechard girl became a victim of the SCIENCE OF MEDICINE. We can consider that a fact. I put up with everything, for I foresaw that if she died anyway, what a terrible torture it would be to have to face the reproach that she would still be alive if the doctors' directions had been followed. This struggle was the hardest for me.

Everything is over, and I am trying hard not to think of the past any more, and gradually I am beginning to acquire some skill in this. So I beg you, Sir, to do me the honor and kindness of visiting me, and, in fact, if it won't inconvenience you, next *Saturday and next Sunday* for supper. You'll find me on a different story, in one of the rooms I used to live in, and Herr Dieterich is with me. We sleep in the same room. Please don't refuse my request. You shall not be troubled by my weeping or complaining — I'm now beyond all that — and whining to my friends has never been my way. So I'll definitely

---

* See following letter. Lichtenberg had met her in 1777, selling flowers, when she was eleven or twelve years old. He gave her work as a kind of maid and taught her the elementary school subjects. In 1780 she moved into his apartment. From then on, they lived as man and wife.

** Albrecht Ludwig Friederich Meister, Professor of Mathematics at the University of Göttingen; formerly Lichtenberg's teacher, then his closest friend among his colleagues.

expect you the day after tomorrow at seven in the evening; I think that all your friends with whom you might have previous engagements would gladly yield to me under the circumstances. The little Dieterich girl would have been twenty-one years old next August 31. If I had only kept my girl that long. She died four years younger.

G. C. L.

TO FRANZ FERDINAND WOLFF[*]

Göttingen, the 19th of August, 1782

Heaven has brought my anxieties to an end, but in a way which has subjected me to great torture, deeply convinced though I am of the infinite wisdom with which it has chosen this way rather than others. The two have died: Mademoiselle Dieterich in her twenty-first year; and she who was my closest concern, a girl of unusual intelligence and heavenly goodness of disposition, whom I had educated completely according to my own ideas, after living seventeen years and thirty-nine days. My sleepless nights and my grief brought on an illness which has kept me prostrate since last Tuesday; I have neither been allowed nor able to get up. Now the machine is moving again: for how long, only He Who was pleased to ruin its movement knows. . . . Very soon you will hear more from

Your most devoted servant,
G. C. Lichtenberg

[*] Met Lichtenberg in Hanover in 1772 and became his friend; they shared their interests in physics and chemistry. (1747–1804)

A Thunderstorm

TO FRANZ FERDINAND WOLFF

Göttingen, July 21st, 1783
4 o'clock in the afternoon

My dear friend,

At just this moment the first snatch of sunshine is appearing again after a frighteningly beautiful thunderstorm with hail; the tiles are still dripping. This time I felt no small anxiety for our town. As the storm approached, it got almost dark and every flash of lightning was a blow. Actually I am not a sentimental sort, at least not in public: I enjoy in silence and let others chatter about it. But truly I am still so full of this great spectacle that the other things I wanted to tell you, which would have been *all* I'd have told you this morning, can't get expressed at all until I've told you something about my feelings. The day was oppressively hot and I was extremely sensitive; moreover, this is the anniversary of my father's death, on which I ordinarily shut myself away. Nothing in the world could correspond better with my feelings than such weather. When the thunder once rolled so deep that I thought it was *under* me, I never, I may say, felt my own nothingness more keenly than in that moment. Truly, tears came to my eyes — tears merely of admiration and heart-felt devotion. There can be nothing greater and more majestic. I don't know—— I now feel unusually light; it is as if I had paid off a great debt and as if the spirit of my father were rejoicing that I observed so unhypocritical an hour of prayer on his anniversary. Now it has been said, and now I am back to my usual pace.

Fortunately the storm moved rapidly. The next peal of thunder followed the lightning in three seconds, so it might well have struck here, but I heard nothing about it. There was only a little hail; no window-pane within my range of vision was broken, but it made quite a clatter on the tiles. The street, though, looked like the Leine.* The pigs look as clean as humans, and the humans, like pigs.

The storm is leaving, and the girls are appearing at the windows vertically.

I have the honor of remaining *in nebula nebulorum*.

G. C. L.

* River on which Göttingen is situated.

Volta

TO FRANZ FERDINAND WOLFF

Göttingen, the 22nd of November, 1784

Dearest Friend,

. . . I do indeed regret that you did not speak to Volta. He is an extraordinary man. DeLuc is right: he wrote me once *qu'en Electricité Volta voyoit avec les yeux de Newton.* He is full of ideas and a *raisonneur* without peer. He had many instruments along; he unpacked them for me, and during his stay here I kept them in my own quarters. They are locksmith's work, but he accomplished everything with them. He stayed here five days, and two-thirds of them, certainly, he spent in my room. My experiments with aerial electricity pleased him incredibly. For I let an 18-inch balloon rise out of the window on a thread of silk woven together with silver and investigated the electricity of the air, on my table, in all ways. I struck suns two inches in diameter. Watching, he was overtaken by his own ideas, and he actually did not hear or see some aristocratic students whom I introduced to him formally. The next day he came at dawn and made preparations to repeat the experiments himself, which he actually did. On that morning the air was so still that the balloon on my balcony hung three hundred feet high, directly above our heads. I had stretched a silk ribbon across the balcony-doorway; the balloon string was wound around this and thus led over to the table. So away with kites in the future, at least for class purposes. I can't stand the field trips with the "fellow-students."

Then he wanted to show me an experiment to prove that fumes carry away positive electricity. He insulated a brazier containing a few dimly glowing coals; wet a linen rag and threw it on the coals; he had run a wire from the brazier to a very sensitive electrometer. But nothing happened. He cursed in French and Italian; but since, as you know, curses are little if any help on such occasions, there was no improvement. That afternoon I repeated the experiments with the *Aeolipia* and then with ether, and they went splendidly. At least I got a *Voyés Vous* for thanks. He is a handsome fellow, and during some extremely uninhibited hours, at a supper at my place when we talked wildly till about one o'clock, I noticed that he has an expert knowledge of the electricity in girls. . . .

I have the honor to remain, with sincere esteem, Sir,

Your most obedient servant,

G. C. Lichtenberg

A Thwarted Plan

TO JOHANN GOTTWERT MÜLLER*

Göttingen, December 20th, 1784

Your short but excellent letter gave me a very great deal of pleasure. As for your friendly sharing in my joy at the journey to Italy, however, I've made a small, permissible change. I have kept its total value but reversed its meaning. Alas, my journey has come to nothing — not only quite without fault of mine, but even with a little loss of five hundred talers. I had money, indeed considerably more than was needed for carriage grease and for oats; I had permission, health, and courage — but my friend and traveling companion, the Danish Finance-Counsellor Ljungberg, of Copenhagen, had not taken enough trouble about arranging for leave. He was kept up in the air, and finally, after I had long since given up all my lecture courses, paid back sixty gleaming louis d'or and waived my claim to forty others, he was refused. I thought I would fall to the floor. In fact, though I have never been out of my mind, I now know how a man feels when he is on the point of frenzy, and that is the only profit I've had in this matter.

I had prepared myself for the journey for more than nine weeks, crossed the Rubicon with Caesar, the Alps with Hannibal, and with Constantine the bridge where the sacred cross stood in the sky. I climbed up the Capitol, touched the prows of the ships and felt giddy on the Tarpeian Rock. — In the second act appeared the Laocoön, the Apollo Belvedere, and the Medicean Venus in

---

* Book dealer in Itzehoe; wrote satirical novels which Lichtenberg greatly admired. (1743–1828)

Florence; all the walls were hung with Raphaels and Correggios. — In the third I clambered up Vesuvius, went for a walk among the Pontine swamps, which have recently been burned over, saw the Styx and the Cave of the Dog, and walked down avenues of blooming aloe and orange trees — and suddenly, as if lightning had struck, nothing was there for my whole winter except Göttingen snow, the ringing of sleigh bells, and the scrawny hyacinth bulbs by my window.

But, friend, the journey is only delayed; next September I'll quite certainly make it if I can find companionship, of which there's no doubt. It has long been my carefully considered axiom: no one who can go there must fail to see Italy. That journey is strength for body and soul.

You were anxious about me because of winter. No, my dear fellow, Italy must be seen in the winter. In the first place, one plays hooky for a whole winter — which is really no trifle for people like us — and goes for walks among the flowers, while certain people in Itzehoe, whom I won't name, admire the lovely icicles in their beards. And then, Italy is really too hot for us in the summer and very unhealthy unless one is willing and able to spend months in some of the *uninteresting* regions. Between Rome and Naples, the orange trees are already along the highways; there, I think, the song, "A Child is Born in Bethlehem, Bethlehem," can be struck up without fuss and foot stoves. If you could come along, dearest friend, what a joy that would be! One ought to have eight-hundred talers (apiece, I mean), and for that we would see Dresden, Prague, Vienna, Trieste, Venice, Milan, Turin, Pavia, Bologna, Florence, Rome, Naples, perhaps Calabria and Messina; on the way back *Loretto,* Lucca, Livorno, the Alps, Geneva, Lausanne, Berne, Zürich, Basle, etc. What a harvest for you, who are cer-

tainly on the way to become our Fielding* — and more!
What psychological views you could collect. For a man
like you, the book dealer must pay the travel costs. . . .

* Henry Fielding, English novelist, author of *Tom Jones*. (1707–1754)

Congratulations to a New Father

TO GEORG HEINRICH HOLLENBERG*

Göttingen, November 13th, 1785

Noble Sir,

Right Honorable General County Surveyor
Praiseworthy, graduated Papa!

Bravo, bravo! dear friend. That's the way. Marriage today and in a year — crash, bang, baptism! What good, otherwise, are all learning and all canal building? Papa Hollenberg — that sounds so splendid to me that I have probably said it ten times today, and once out the window, so that all the world could have heard it. — Oh, do write me how you look now! Is it really true that when a man becomes a papa he must acquire a big peruke, wear a figured dressing-gown, and a belt, and yellow slippers and at times stand in the window with his long pipe in his mouth and his pipe tamper on his little finger; and whether another dressing gown is needed for Sundays; also, whether he must cross the street more slowly than before, and how much time you now need, say, to go from the gate of the Kaiser Inn to the new city-hall stairs; and whether he may read the evening blessing in the same tone as before without coughing when he begins; and whether at night he has to sleep on the side of the bed where the cradle is standing, or whether he may lie down on the far side next to the wall; and whether it is absolutely necessary to be a model for the servants in the house, especially the maids, with earnest

---

* Ten years younger than Lichtenberg; was a civil engineer in Osnabrück when Lichtenberg stayed there in 1772.

face and good example? You see, my dear fellow, these
are cardinal questions which, if they are properly answered in my case, might yet bring me some day to the
position where you now are.*

All joking aside, my dear Hollenberg, your letter
really gave me a pleasure which moved me to tears. I
see that you are happy; what you have told me of your
admirable wife proves this beyond contradiction, and I
take so much real interest in everything that concerns
you that your happiness always constitutes no small part
of mine. Keep your fondness for me as it has been, and
gain me the friendship of your wife, who must be high-
minded, from the few lines I have seen. And if some day
you are again delighted by a little girl who is heavier
by half an ounce or so — that's what we wicked unmarried sinners call the little boys — then dedicate this
puellam cum appendice to

Your

most faithful friend

G. C. Lichtenberg

* Written tongue-in-cheek: The birth of Lichtenberg's first child by Margarete Kellner, his common-law wife, was less than three months away.
Georg Christoph, Jr., was born on February 4, 1786.

The Good Life

TO GOTTFRIED HIERONYMUS AMELUNG *

Göttingen, March 24th, 1786

My best friend!

I give you this name with all the fullness of my heart, for none of my friends, not excepting even my brothers, treat my inexcusable negligence in letter-writing with the heavenly forbearance with which you deal with it. You can't believe how great the very particular emotion was with which, therefore, I read your excellent essay in the *Church Herald* about a week ago. At every line I thought: Look, what an excellent man you have offended. I was also really on the point of asking you for your absolution in a circumstantial confession, when your kind letter came; it revived my spirits and gave me assurance that I could again write directly to my Amelung without making this tiresome confession of my sins.

Yet I do owe you the following confession: I have a great deal to do, even though I lecture only three hours a day. The nature of my lectures does not require the usual preparation, like dogmatics, say, or Pandects, etc. Rather, the numerous instruments which have been unused for half a year often have to be looked for among the great many we own; they must be properly set up when they are found, and frequently even repaired, for there are some at which the tooth of time, and those of the mice and moths, very soon begin to gnaw — not even to mention the fingers and elbows of the ignorant servants. Thus the days pass. Moreover, my friends here

* One of Lichtenberg's schoolmates, who became a minister.

who know my duties also know which hours I am free, for which I am very grateful to them, and visit me on Sundays or in the evenings. When I am alone I am frequently very tired, or find myself obliged to catch up with the latest achievements in my field, lest I fall behind. Seldom, anyway, am I in the proper mood without which one must never write to Amelung. You see, that's about how things are with me — forgive me.

What is my dear little friend up to? Is he already falling nicely? And breaking things nicely? The former is a very good sign, only one must try to arrange that it always takes place on his behind, which exists mainly for that purpose. While I don't grasp the psychological reason, it is certain that man is an animal which must, if it is to reach its destination, be attacked first at its behind, until its 10th year, and then at its head. I conceive of behind and head as the poles of the magnetic needle, which, however opposed to each other they may be, have yet a great affinity between them. — What can I send the dear little fellow? Just tell me. You know our exports: sausage and compendia. Would they be welcome? Say the word!

The ideas you expressed about religion and — THEOLOGY in your last letter to me pleased me vastly. They are so very much my own that I could almost believe that you had looked into my Ledger, in which I usually enter my little intellectual income penny by penny, every day. But of course a man of your intellect and active benevolence, the sort which can exist only where there's sincere conviction, does not need to look into the ledger of a professor — and a layman at that! — to learn such things. Meanwhile, quiet in the harbor, I calmly watch all the troubles of life and am convinced that after all they finally *help* to lead us toward the great goal of our true destiny. Since we cannot see very far beyond our own position, the best way can be found only through experiments. With this method, to be sure, many a man will perish in the morass which his successor will avoid just because he has perished there. In the long run everything will be clear and good, if only we love one another, and each one, with practised understanding, tries to do as much good as he can. If I were ever to publish a sermon, it would certainly be about the great ability that everyone, be he who he will, has to do good, without wasting anything. People of all stations, all over the world, fail to realize their importance in this respect. In this regard, everyone, whoever he is, is a prince in his own situation. The devil take our existence here on earth if only the Emperor could do good. That is the Law and the Prophets. Something of this, I think, ought to be included in every sermon. You are the man who shows this through his example: what an impression would it not make, if you taught this from the pulpit and demonstrated in DETAIL how everyone could play a similar part in his own situation!

Now an affair which occurred three nights before last in our house and is indeed completely unprecedented here and really terrible. It took place on my story, but since I live in one of the largest houses of the town, it happened so far from me that I heard nothing at all of the thing while it was going on. In this story a Count Breuner of Vienna, the son of the Imperial Ambassador to the Republic of Venice, has accommodations with his tutor, Captain Burdell; both are men of the highest character. They wanted to depart at Easter, and received last week their monies for the journey and for paying their bill, about 2,000 talers in louis d'or at five. The rabble here found out about this; generally it acquires information very much faster than do the leaders of our police. So on the night mentioned, six or seven masked fellows broke into the Captain's room, tied him up in bed with ripped-up curtains, hunted the keys quite calmly, and escaped with all the money, after threatening to set the house on fire if he made the slightest noise. Actually the rug did start to burn, which fire the Captain, who hurled himself out of the bed, rolled out with his own body. — Isn't this a hideous affair, especially in a house in which at least fifty to sixty people are asleep, and in a sleepy little place like Göttingen?

Holland and the Seashore

TO GOTTFRIED HIERONYMUS AMELUNG

Göttingen, April 21st, 1786

... What life is like here, how one is bothered here, what loss of time is caused by labors to which one has committed oneself, you can't believe. Occasionally I brood about myself for a week and have leisure and indeed do what I will; and then when the time comes that I would like to do what I intended, there is so much I *must* do that I hardly remember who I am.

Please give my greetings to your family; it must be a splendid one in every respect. I hope to visit you *in loco* before I die; it is with this hope that I console myself during my present tied-down oyster life.

I have few if any acquaintances in Holland. I don't love the people there. The cities are splendid, and you will see installations there, the kind one dreams of. There is no considerable city in Holland which I have not seen. I have examined their shipping and their houses, but their inhabitants, excepting some scholars, struck me as unbearable. They cut a very poor figure beside the English. A man who goes to Holland from England thinks that he has been shifted from a society of well-bred officers to drummer boys and military police.

If you want to see the sea in its full *lustre,* don't fail to visit Scheveningen or Schevelingen, one hour from The Hague, at the end of a pleasant wood, almost the only one in Holland. The view is splendid because there are no islands lying opposite nor does any deep harbor hide it with the multitude of its ships. But, dearest friend, do try at least a little voyage, at least ten or twelve miles from the shore, even if only on a fishing boat. There you will see things of which an inlander simply can't form a conception. I have been at sea six times, once in danger; but in the year 1778, when I was not in danger though the wind blew hard, I saw a sight which I'll never forget. The wind piled up high waves, shell-shaped deep hollows, which were easily thirty or forty feet long; above, our ship hovered safely but like a straw. I stood on the deck and had tied myself to the main-mast with a rope. I have never seen anything grander. The irresistibility of the whole, the human boldness and the spirit manifest in it, combined with the thunder of the waves — for what one hears from afar is real thunder — actually forced from me tears (I do not know how to describe them) of reverence, of ecstasy, or of humiliation before the great Creator. In the cabin lay people who thought that the end was near. There is no grander view in nature. . . .

A Fire

TO JOHANN DANIEL RAMBERG*

Göttingen, August 6th, 1786

Noble Sir,

... Now one more small but sad affair, of which I am still much too full to keep quiet about. In the night from August 4 to 5, I was awakened at 12:30 by the cry of *Fire!* When I opened my eyes, my bedroom was as bright as if the sun were shining, and before I could locate the sleeves of my dressing-gown, the color rose to a pinkish red. It was directly opposite me. But I quickly got hold of myself, ran for my bit of money, and only then looked into the matter further: I found the gable of a house wrapped in flames, and I felt the warmth. There was little wind, however, and what little there was, was favorable to me, so I ordered that none of my things were to be saved, and it turned out fortunately. A hose operated by an air-chamber worked so splendidly that I laughed and shed tears of joy; it was a strange sensation.

On this occasion I found an observation confirmed which I had already made before. The danger of fire, and perhaps and presumably every danger, is more terrible to the imagination than *in re;* we usually think of such things when body and soul are ill disposed. When the danger is actually at hand, brooding, the product of coddling and idleness, disappears, and one becomes a man of action who keeps his eye only on *res facti*. I was cautious and alert, completely calm, and ready for all eventualities.

* Army Counselor in Hanover, Lichtenberg's friend from 1772 on.

I was uncommonly pleased that the princes'* tutors came to my room and stayed till the end. The next morning princes and tutors sent inquiries about how I was, and when the princes were passing by the following evening and I was leaning out of the window, they rushed up below it and called up to me about the incident. They themselves were wisely allowed to sleep through it, for though they dwell in the same building as I, their quarters face on another street. . . .

* King George III's three younger sons studied at the University of Göttingen. They had been introduced to Lichtenberg as children, in 1775, when he was a guest of the king's family. Now he lectured to them privately six times a week. Two of the princes roomed in Dieterich's large house, where Lichtenberg was also a tenant.

A Message to a God-child

TO GEORG HEINRICH HOLLENBERG

Göttingen, the 23rd of September, 1788
Dearest Friend,

For Heaven's sake, don't interpret it as negligence that I am rather late in answering your valued letter. Actually I should have said: my dear, kind friend, explain to your beloved wife that the slight delay of my answer does not stem from negligence. For *you* know me, I know, and you know how much everything which concerns you interests me, and how much I am pleased by each incident which brings me into a closer relation with you and your family.

Long live the *Dauphin, Bernhard the First,* and his gallant parents, therefore, and a thousand thanks for the honor of being made godfather. I actually wanted to write to the little fellow himself, and I did not consider till very late that he would hardly be able to read the letter. It began thus: Welcome, dear little one, in this vale of tears! I am uncommonly pleased to see you here. But be careful: you can't possibly believe what a hole it is, this world. If you want to be happy, for Heaven's sake stay on the highway with your wagon; otherwise you will run the risk that the priests will unharness your horses, and there you will sit. *Or more briefly:* act in all respects like your worthy father and in as few as possible like your worthy godfather; then you can't go wrong. Moreover, don't cry too much. Be quiet especially at night, and bear in mind that your good mother wants to sleep too, and that during the day, when you're asleep, she has other things to do.

When you begin to walk, I, of course, allow you to fall down, for a regular boy falls at least three times a day. But just don't fall on your so-called pate, for *that* God gave you to write compendia; and not on your nose, for that serves to set spectacles on. Rather you will soon find that Nature equipped you in the middle of your body (N.B., towards the rear) with two cushions, which are called buttocks. Look, dear boy, these two things have no use in the world except the following, which can conveniently be arranged in four groups:

1) During the study of the Latin language and of Christianity, or when naughty, in the beginning to be whacked with the hand, and in more mature years with the rod.

2) To fall on it. So when you notice that you would fall on your head, you make a leap and fall on your respective falling-mats.

3) To let yourself down on them or, as one says, to sit down. For since the chairs of the Patriarchs were of wood or stone, Nature had to attach the cushions to the body. Today, when people, the upper class particularly, frequently lose these natural pillows, buttocks have been attached to the chairs themselves.

4) And that is a principal use. If some nasty fellow is reviling you and does not even have the guts to stand up to you until you've been able to box his ears, open your coat in the rear and show him your cushions. In learned controversies, this type of self-defense is not valid; scholars have a very special backside, usually called *moral,* which does not lie at the center of their system. How people show it to each other, you will learn at the universities, where there is abundant oppor-

tunity for mutual instruction; this science is called polemics.

Dearest friend, excuse me for this little joke; it was inspired only by the joy caused by your admirable letter, which is lying open before me; I could give you no better evidence of the sincerity of my feelings than the sort I furnished. For even "Guides for Letter Writers" have the *words* for an answer, just as today buttocks of deer and horse hair and eiderdown are buckled on the chairs and armchairs; yet lack of feeling cannot be replaced by affectation. . . .

Now, dearest friend, give my most cordial regards to your dear wife and to the *Dauphin*. I remain, in true friendship and devotion, always

Yours,

G. C. Lichtenberg

News From Home

TO JOHANN CHRISTIAN DIETERICH

Göttingen, the 26th of May, 1791! Well, what sort of a beginning of a letter is that! you will say. To give to the date, which stands there only for the letter's sake, such an appearance of *We by the Grace of God,* as if the letter were there only for its sake — that is indeed against the eternal laws of letter-writing. You are right, my dear Dieterich. But "hereby hangs a tale," the English say; that is, a very great deal could be said about it, and today I lack patience and time for just that, precisely because it's the 26th of May. So I'll only tell you that this day is always one of the most agreeable of the whole year to me, since it is the birthday of a man whom I love as I do my own life. It is for this reason that, when I am permitted to drink wine, I always drink rather more, with my wife and children, on this day than at other times, don't walk or sit as at other times, and always date my letters as if the letter were there for the date's sake. Do you understand now, old fellow? Good. That was the date; now comes the letter.

Well, first some news and indeed the bad news first: last Saturday morning at 11 Meyenberg* died, and the next day at just this time our excellent Murray.** The former lay sick for some days, unable to speak and without any perceptions, but the latter is said to have kept his intellectual powers till the last moment. The jurist-mayor was dissected, at his express desire; the doc-

---

* Georg Philipp Meyenberg, Mayor of Göttingen.

** Johann Andreas Murray, Professor of Medicine at the University of Göttingen.

tor, however, was *not* — likewise at his desire. It was
splendid of our generous Richter * to offer his help spon-
taneously to Murray, who, as is well-known, realized
everything about his illness. He really did visit him. It
was too late, to be sure, but Murray would surely have
considered an earlier visit the worst of insults. This gallant man was buried today. When I saw Wrisberg* going
there in black clothing and Richter driving there from a
distance, my chest felt rather constricted, I confess, and
tears rose to my eyes. I went away from the window and
restored my cheerfulness again.

Now the pleasant news: your dear wife and children, my dear wife and children, and I all look and
stand as vigorously as your gardens; at times I look almost as green too. Yet I am well nevertheless and think
that when autumn and winter arrive, the yellowness will
come of itself; these are trivial matters. Now I have 2 or
3 over 100 in my lectures, from which I conclude that
the number of new arrivals must be considerable.

Well, this is enough for today, perhaps I'll write
again soon. Be sure to arrange to be here again soon,
at the latest for Saturday before Pentecost. Your garden
is waiting for you in all its glory. At least once a day I
rejoice in the splendid sight; if it weren't for the privet
hedges, the odor of the fresh leaves and the flowers
could be smelled in my study, I think. My dear wife and
children kiss and embrace you, and the 26th of May is
really shining in their eyes already (7 o'clock in the
morning) while I am writing this. When you went away
my boy had 4 bandages on his body, now he has 6 of
them, it's getting better every day. On Sunday he was
fated to get his first box on the ears from a ragamuffin

* August Gottlob Richter and Heinrich August Wrisberg were professors
of Medicine at the University of Göttingen; Richter was Lichtenberg's family
doctor.

on the highway — and he had deserved it — which shows consistency at least. Remember me to your respected son and all good friends, and while in Gotha take good care of your and my own affairs.

Your faithful

G. C. Lichtenberg

To a Little Boy

TO GEORG HEINRICH HOLLENBERG

Göttingen, September 2nd, 1793

Dearest friend,

You must by all means forgive me if I do not honor every draft which your love draws on me in the currency which you demand. I mean, if I don't immediately answer your letters with letters. The hardest thing for my heart is to raise precisely this sort of conventional money. If you would visit me some day, man closest to my heart, I would tell you stories, read to you, wait on you hand and foot; I would kiss your dear children and, with the permission of the authorities, your charming wife too. I would do and say a thousand things, and have a thousand done and said, from which you could tell how much I love you and with what precision I answer your letters, in silent gratitude. But to write letters, *write* with pen and ink on paper, that, that, you wonderful fellow, is as hard for me at times as jumping over a fence. But of course if it goes on that way, one must——

Yet for this a new, clean sheet is needed,
so turn over.

Dear little Hermann Hollenberg, I send you a thousand greetings because of your fine parents, whom I love and whom you are bringing so much joy and, if you are obedient, will continue to do so. But allow a few words to me, an old friend of your worthy father and one who has some acquaintance with the world. I see that you have no trousers on; men of that sort are now called *sans culottes;* and by that, people in many sections of your German fatherland mean the Satan's spawn of liberal intellectuals, philosophers, teachers of the people, and free-thinkers — in a word, all those who do not devote themselves to chasing golden snuff-boxes.* Now although it's no disgrace to come into the world without trousers, as you did — or, like your father's friend, soon to leave it without having any on — do cover your nakedness with this necessary garment as long as you wander about in this world. Have it so cut that if possible it will cover your eyes and ears, and wear your head inside your fly too, and then you will never want for anything. Above all things, though, my dearest child, endeavor — My God, what am I saying? I didn't stop to think that it is no longer wise to dispatch truths by mail, so the rest orally some day. Oh! joking aside, your domestic happiness has meant a thoroughly lovely charming evening for me. If only I had the patience and energy to write!

For hours I have been looking for your last letter to answer some points raised in it; with my impatient nature I've been unable to find it. Since just today I am somewhat in the mood to write, the letters are crowding upon me so terribly that I must close. Remember me to the dear new mother, and your little *sans culottes* Arminius, and all the others most cordially, and do not forget me,

Your

faithful

G. C. Lichtenberg

* Presumably given by one's superiors as tokens of recognition.

After an Illness

TO JOHANN GOTTWERT MÜLLER

Göttingen, July 16th, 1794

Honored Sir and Friend,

I don't know whether you have heard that at the very time, even on almost the same day, that the revolution broke out in France a most remarkable one broke out in my body and my domestic life. I got married,* and that is the fine side of the upheaval; I was attacked by a convulsive asthma which threatened me with suffocation almost daily for more than four weeks, that is the ugly side. On the first part I will say no more, dearest friend, than that I live most happily and pleasantly, and have four children running about me, who, thank God, are all very healthy. With my admirable wife they make my life so very delightful that I look back on the portion of it when I could have been married but was not, as on a half-savage state. This goes so far that, just as Cato used to end his letters with *Carthaginem esse delendam,* I always end mine to unmarried friends with *uxorem esse ducendam.***

But of the second part, my dear friend, I have more to say. If it had been only a matter of the four aforesaid weeks, I would barely have mentioned it and by no means would have called it a revolution. After that attack I was bedridden, and was lying down literally a full half year of $365 \div 2$ days, lived mainly on medicines at that time, did recover, to be sure, but how? *Eheu*

---

* See introduction, page 27.
** "A man must marry," a parody of "We must destroy Carthage."

quantum mutatus ab illo! * Truly our transfigured body, on the day of resurrection, cannot be as different from the buried bag of maggots in the earth as the reconvalescent *Hofrat* was from the one who had been put to bed 365 ÷ 2 days before. Only with the vast difference that the transfigured one stayed in bed and the bag of maggots got up. My gaiety, my fearlessness, my carefreeness, my love of reading and of writing at least for myself, all that stayed in bed and now is gone.

All my present life seems to me so lacking in coherence in itself and with its earlier portion that you would hardly take it for the index of what preceded it, if you looked at it through my eyes. I began to consider myself as an entirely different person and literally believed that the bag of maggots was not obliged to pay the debts which the transfigured one had contracted. So my whole correspondence began to come to a halt. When I still wrote letters, they were always those in which something appeared, at least in the postscript, which served to feed the *fire* in the *kitchen,* or where I could have been prosecuted legally for dilatoriness. The pen from which many a joke for my friends used to flow, now produced almost nothing anymore but *valutas, usances* and *at sights;*** at least I don't know how to express more briefly what it wrote than by these words, the most unaesthetic I can imagine. Here, best of men, you have the data for an introduction to this renewed correspondence with you, which † I do not wish to pursue further now. I shall add only this one thing, that I find my condition VERY, VERY much more tolerable in this fertile year of storms and have hope that I shall be reborn.

---

* "Alas, how much he has changed!" In the *Aeneid,* Aeneas says this of the dead Hector, who appears to him in a dream.

** Terms used in writing out bills of exchange and notes.

† *Videlicet* the introduction, not the correspondence. *Videatur contextus.*

You, good man, warm friend, and (German) FIELDING * have never been absent from my heart, either after my resurrection or before my decease. I read your letter not without deep emotion. If Dieterich had been here then (I could not write a complete answer in his absence) I would have answered at once, but he stayed away for a long time. When he came, my dreadful indolence set in again with the southing-hot (I meant to write "seething hot," but let it stand) weather, and so the answer was not written until today. Now your excellent friend volunteers to take it to you.

Dieterich is certainly your friend now as ever. A certain negligence, which has always been characteristic of him, and a certain failing of his memory, in which alone his old age shows, and all sorts of domestic circumstances of the saddest sort have occasioned several stoppages like the one between you and him. Thank God, however, the prosperity of his business has not decreased. He is ineffably devoted to you and believes that you had forgotten him. Please don't forget him, and bless his press again. I know that he will eagerly pick up even the crumbs which fall from your table, for it hurt him a great deal when you sent your delicacies to Berlin and Stettin.** If you wish to admit him to favor again, do let me handle the matter.

Truly, dearest friend, I am astonished at the inexhaustibility of your genius. In little Itzehoe, you carry a whole London in your head. Do tell me how you manage that and what sort of Herschelian *** invention you have made, so that in the little town where you live you look so deeply and rightly into the world that

---

* Lichtenberg compares Müller to the English novelist.
** Towns where some of Müller's books were published.
*** In 1781, when still an unknown astronomer, Sir William Herschel (1738–1822) discovered the planet Uranus with a telescope of his own construction. This and his subsequent discoveries attracted world-wide attention.

its circumnavigators lag behind you. Perhaps I shall take occasion very soon to express publicly, even if only in a few hasty lines, thanks for the pleasure you have afforded me. To be sure, it will not be done merely out of gratitude but (this is only whispered) to tell the public that I know this man and that he is my friend.

What is my dear godson up to? Is he coming to Göttingen soon?

Well, my dearest friend, remember me to your estimable wife, of whose praise everyone who comes from there is full, and remain the friend of

Your

always faithful

G. C. Lichtenberg

To Herr Fielding-Müller

Lichtenberg's Last Letter

TO LUDWIG CHRISTIAN LICHTENBERG*

Göttingen, the 18th of February, 1799

My dear brother,

... Your anti-Kantianism really delighted me, since I know now how you see the matter. As a person he is certainly a great man — and what is certainly just as important, a well-intentioned, worthy one. His *Critique of Pure Reason* is the work of 30 years of study. He has given lectures on systems of philosophy for a long time; this, to be sure, made him familiar with a great many things with which countless people, even men of real intellect, are not — at least not to the same degree. Therefore he often does not seem to be clear until one becomes familiar with his thought. Therefore even K——** often knows nothing to adduce against him except that Leibniz, say, said something similar 100 years ago. But Kant does not pass himself off as the discoverer of everything either; he only interrelates what great men said and thought singly long ago, and (N.B.) shows why we must think and speak in that way. It's well known that Aristarchus of Samos taught, more than 1000 years before Copernicus, that the sun stood still and the earth revolved about it, but those were only single rays of light which were lost in the surrounding waste of darkness. Kant once alludes to some such matter — in the preface to his *Critique of Pure Reason,* if I'm not mis-

* One of Lichtenberg's older brothers.
** A. G. Kästner (1719–1800), Professor of Mathematics at Göttingen and Lichtenberg's teacher, wrote satirical epigrams. He was disliked by Lichtenberg and many others for his vanity and his domineering manner.

taken — with great delicacy. The comparison stands up. Up to now we have believed that we were the product of things outside of us, of which we knew and could know, after all, nothing except what our Ego reported to us. What, then, if it were precisely the nature of our being that actually makes this world? Here the revolving and rotation of the earth around its axis are opposed to the revolving of the sun and the host of stars around it. Indeed, he puts everything to the test. A dogmatizing Kantian is surely not a genuine one. Even Fichte, *quod pace tua dixerim,** has offended more against discretion than against philosophy. It was culpable mischievousness in him, it seems to me, to speak the way he did, and will probably always be. We more refined Christians look down upon the worship of images; i.e., our God does not consist of wood and tinsel, but He always remains an image, which is only another member of precisely the same series — subtler, but always an image. If the spirit of man wants to tear itself away from this worship of images, it finally arrives at the Kantian idea. But it is arrogance to believe that as mixed a being as man will ever acknowledge all that PURELY. Therefore, all that the really wise man can do is to guide everything towards a good goal, and yet to take men *as they are*. Of this Herr Fichte seems to understand nothing, and in this respect he is a rash and foolish man. — Forgive me, dear brother, I went further today than I intended. That's what happens when one's heart has a word to say too.

   Adieu, adieu.

                                        G. C. L.

---

* "If you don't mind my saying so"

Selected Bibliography

Lichtenberg's Writings:

Vermischte Schriften. 9 volumes. Göttingen: 1800–1806.
Vermischte Schriften. Vollständige Originalausgabe. 8 volumes. Göttingen: 1844–1847.
Aphorismen. ed. Leitzmann. 5 volumes. Berlin: B. Behr, 1902–1908.
Briefe. ed. Leitzmann and Schüddekopf. 3 volumes. Leipzig: Dieterich, 1901–1904.
Reflections. sel. and tr. Alliston. London: Sonnenschein, 1908.
Mare, Margaret L. and Quarrel, W. H. *Lichtenberg's Visits to England.* Oxford: Clarendon Press, 1938.

Literature:

Grenzmann, W. *Georg Christoph Lichtenberg.* Salzburg and Leipzig: Pustet, 1939.
Mautner, F. H. "Amintors Morgenandacht," *Deutsche Vierteljahrsschrift für Literaturwissenschaft,* 30 (1956), 401–416.
———. "Lichtenberg as an Interpreter of Hogarth," *Modern Language Quarterly,* 13 (1952) 64–80.
———. "Lichtenbergs Anfänge in ihren Wesenszügen," *PMLA* (Publications of the Modern Language Association of America), 41 (1941), 671–709.
———. "Lichtenbergs ungedruckte Tagebücher," *Euphorion,* 51 (1957), 23–41.
———. and Miller, Franklin. "Remarks on G. C. Lichtenberg, Humanist-Scientist," *Isis,* 43/3 (1952), 223–232.
Requadt, P. *Lichtenberg.* Hameln: Seifert, 1946.
Schneider, A. *G. C. Lichtenberg, Précurseur du Romantisme.* Nancy: Société d'Impressions Typographiques, 1954.
———. *Georg Christoph Lichtenberg, Penseur.* Paris: Société d'Edition "Les Belles Lettres," no date.
Schöffler, H. *Lichtenberg.* Göttingen: Vandenhoeck & Ruprecht, 1956.
von Wright, G. H. "Georg Christoph Lichtenberg als Philosoph," *Theoria,* 8 (1942), 201–217.

Sources of Aphorisms

References designated by capital letters indicate Leitzmann's edition; Roman numerals, the *Vermischte Schriften* of 1844–1847; *PhM,* the *Physikalisch-Mathematische Schriften* in the *Vermischte Schriften,* nine-volume edition of 1800–1806.